I0815223

FROM PALMA TO PRINCETON

STUDY ROOM

From Palma to Princeton
Unraveling the Mystery of a Mallorcan Stairway

ALEXANDRA LETVIN
ELENA TOROK

Princeton University Art Museum
Distributed by Princeton University Press
Princeton and Oxford

Contents

Foreword

One of the largest single works of art in Princeton's collections, the Mallorcan stairway and gallery—long known as the Spanish Stairs—was among the first to grace the Princeton University Art Museum's new building, opened in October 2025. Its removal and eventual reinstallation were two of the most complex aspects of that multi-year capital project. In 2021 the entire ensemble, weighing more than twenty-one thousand pounds, was disassembled and removed from the old Museum, where it had initially been installed in 1965. It was transported to Maryland for a lengthy conservation treatment, returned to Princeton, and reinstalled in fall 2024 as one of the most important objects physically embedded in the new building.

Visitors familiar with our previous building will recall the architectural ensemble from the former galleries of medieval, Byzantine, and Islamic art, where the stairway element led generations of Princeton students to the works on paper study room and some of the balustrades and columns—originally part of an upper-level residential gallery, or "loggia"—physically demarcated the gallery spaces. The multifaceted project of deinstalling, conserving, and reinstalling the elements spurred new research and discoveries that transformed how they are presented to the public in our new space, where they "face off" with the building's own Grand Stair.

It is fitting, then, that this magnificent architectural ensemble serves as the subject of the first book in the Museum's new publication series, Study Room. Written to appeal to both general and academic audiences, these attractively priced volumes will offer deep looks at key works from the Museum's collections, placing them in context and typically drawing on the expertise of more than one contributor. The goal of the series is to reflect the rich array of artworks as well as the wide-ranging scholarly resources of a university art museum; to provide focused, interdisciplinary investigations of essential works in the Museum's collections; and to present diverse approaches to studying important works of art.

Perhaps because the Mallorcan stairway and gallery were so strongly associated with the Museum as it was reshaped with the opening of its new building in 1966 and with the northern Italian Gothic Revival language of the 1923 building by Ralph Adams Cram that survived that reshaping, relatively little had been known about their origins. While they were long thought to have come from a single residence dating to 1549, research presented here by Alexandra Letvin, who serves as the Museum's inaugural Duane Wilder, Class of 1951, Associate Curator of European Art, and Elena Torok, our first objects conservator, reveals that they adorned at least two different grand residences in Palma de Mallorca and were combined only in the early twentieth century to create an appealing architectural ensemble for the international art market. Letvin's essay introduces the transatlantic network of dealers, restorers, and collectors who played a role in the stairway and gallery's journey from Palma to Princeton; Torok's essay reveals how these individuals altered and reinterpreted these architectural elements over more than one hundred years. Together, the essays offer fresh insight into one of Princeton's most familiar works, now installed as the centerpiece of the Nancy A. Nasher–David J. Haemisegger Family Hall and Grand Stair. Newly conserved, the stairway and gallery stand ready to welcome Museum visitors at a critical moment in their discovery of Princeton's landmark new building.

James Christen Steward
Nancy A. Nasher–David J. Haemisegger, Class of 1976, Director

Introduction

ALEXANDRA LETVIN

An impressive architectural ensemble comprising a stone stairway, balustrades, and columns greets visitors to the Entrance Hall of the Princeton University Art Museum (see pp. 72–73). Together these elements offer a rare surviving example of a classic feature of fifteenth- and sixteenth-century stately residences, or *casas señoriales*, in the Mediterranean island city of Palma de Mallorca: the interior patio, in which an outdoor stairway leads to a second-story open-air gallery lined with balustrades and often columns {1}. A 1955 gift to the Museum from Baroness Cassel van Doorn, a European émigré to New Jersey, Princeton's patio elements—affectionately known as the Spanish Stairs—served both an aesthetic and a functional purpose in the Museum's gallery of medieval art for more than fifty years {2}. In 2021, in preparation for the construction of the Museum's new building, the patio elements—referred to throughout this volume as the Mallorcan stairway and gallery—were carefully deinstalled. Collectively weighing more than twenty-one thousand pounds, the individual stones were packed into twenty-one crates and transported in three semitrucks to EverGreene Architectural Arts in Maryland, where they underwent a multiyear conservation treatment. As this work unfolded and plans developed for the stairway and gallery to be installed in the Museum's new building, questions about their origins began to emerge.

Although the ensemble had been on continuous display for decades, the Mallorcan stairway and gallery were so seamlessly integrated into the fabric of the 1965 Museum building that little attention had been given to their history or provenance: where they came from and how they came to be at Princeton.[1] The Museum's internal records offered few leads for tracing this history. The accession card documenting the stairway and gallery's entrance into the collections noted only that it was "Acquired (by auction gallery?) from Mr. Arthur Byne of Madrid, Spain, on September 19, 1929" {3}. The sparse curatorial file provided additional intriguing—if apparently conflicting—clues. Four photographs of drawings showed the elements in a different arrangement from their 1965 installation at Princeton (see figs. 42–45). They are accompanied by an introductory sheet with Arthur Byne's name and an inventory number—"S/B Lot #275, Art. #1 to 65"—with no connection to the Art Museum's cataloging system {4}. Additionally, three architectural blueprints dated September 1942 for an alteration and addition to the residence of Baron and Baroness Cassel van Doorn at 240 Broad Avenue in Englewood, New Jersey, depict the elements in yet another configuration (see figs. 61–63).

These disparate pieces of information and the evidence of the stones themselves guided cross-disciplinary research that allowed for the history of the Mallorcan stairway and gallery and its journey to Princeton to come into focus. The resulting transatlantic narrative begins in fifteenth-century Mallorca and ends in twenty-first-century New Jersey. It brings together well-known figures of the twentieth-century art world such as William Randolph Hearst with lesser-known ones such as Arthur Byne, Josep Costa Ferrer, and Baron and Baroness Cassel van Doorn, revealing how the interventions of dealers, restorers,

{1}
Miguel Joarizti and Heribert Mariezcurrena, "Patio de la casa del Conde Ayamans," photoengraving in Pablo Piferrer and José María Quadrado, *Islas Baleares*, vol. 27 of *España: Sus monumentos y artes, su naturaleza e historia* (Barcelona, 1888)

{2}
Mallorcan stairway and gallery, installed in the Princeton University Art Museum, McCormick Hall, after 1966

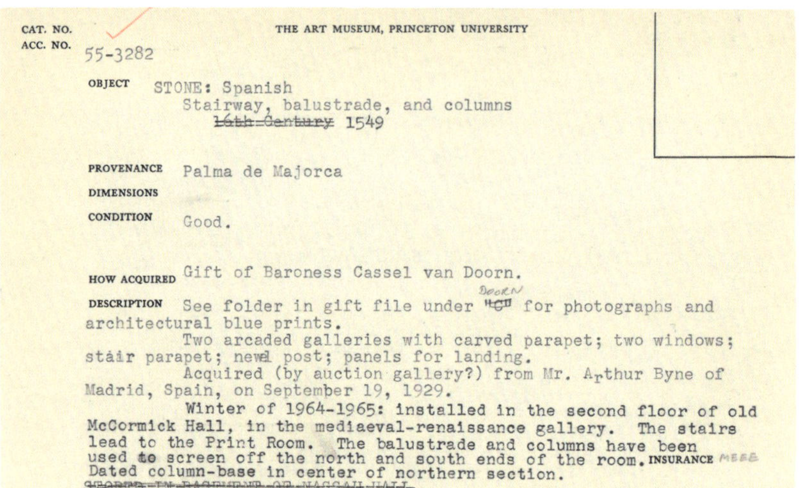

CAT. NO. ACC. NO. 55-3282

THE ART MUSEUM, PRINCETON UNIVERSITY

OBJECT STONE: Spanish
Stairway, balustrade, and columns
~~16th Century~~ 1549

PROVENANCE Palma de Majorca

DIMENSIONS

CONDITION Good.

HOW ACQUIRED Gift of Baroness Cassel van Doorn.

DESCRIPTION See folder in gift file under ~~"C"~~ Doorn for photographs and architectural blue prints.
Two arcaded galleries with carved parapet; two windows; stair parapet; newel post; panels for landing.
Acquired (by auction gallery?) from Mr. Arthur Byne of Madrid, Spain, on September 19, 1929.
Winter of 1964-1965: installed in the second floor of old McCormick Hall, in the mediaeval-renaissance gallery. The stairs lead to the Print Room. The balustrade and columns have been used ~~to~~ screen off the north and south ends of the room. Dated column-base in center of northern section.
~~STORED IN BASEMENT OF NASSAU HALL~~

INSURANCE

{3}
Accession card for the Mallorcan stairway and gallery, 1955. Princeton University Art Museum, Curatorial Files

collectors, and museums can—intentionally or unintentionally—fundamentally change and obscure an object's appearance, meaning, and history. This wide-ranging story is detailed in the two essays that follow. The first introduces the individuals throughout the twentieth century who facilitated the journey of the stairway and gallery to Princeton; the second essay reveals how these individuals restored and reconfigured these elements and, in the process, reinterpreted them.

Mallorca

While long referred to as the Spanish Stairs, Princeton's architectural elements came not from mainland Spain but rather from the island of Mallorca. Along with Ibiza, Menorca, and Formentera, Mallorca is part of the archipelago off the eastern coast of Spain known as the Balearic Islands. Although it has long been part of Spain, it has a rich and distinct identity shaped by its medieval history and a strategic location in the Mediterranean Sea that made it an important crossroads for trade, linking Africa with Europe and the Mediterranean with the Atlantic Ocean {5}.

Mallorca had been controlled by a series of Muslim rulers since 902. In 1229 James I, the Catholic king of Aragon, wrested power over the island from the Almohad Caliphate, a North African Berber Muslim empire.[2] When James I died in 1276, his will divided his vast territories between two sons: Peter inherited the mainland Kingdoms of Aragon and Valencia and the Principality of Catalonia; James

{4}
The lot description accompanying four photographs of now-lost drawings made by Arthur Byne in 1929, from the International Studio Art Corporation's Inventory Album 83. Princeton University Art Museum, Curatorial Files

19

S/B LOT #275 - ART. #1 to 65

This is No. 1 of 4 photographs
- showing main view of -

THE MAJORCAN PATIO AND STAIRWAY FROM
PALMA DE MAJORCA, SPAIN

SPANISH .... XVI CENTURY

Consisting of two Arcaded Galleries with carved Parapet, two stone windows, a Gothic stone parapet, newel post and several perforated panels of the landing.

Acquired from Mr. Arthur Byne, Madrid, Spain 9/19/29

Note: The ceiling shown in this photograph was not included in this lot.

A -
C - (ANYY)

sold

CLASSIFICATION: BUILDINGS AND PARTS I.S.A.C.

{5}
Map of the western Mediterranean

(known as James II of Mallorca) was given the newly created Kingdom of Mallorca, which comprised the Balearic Islands, the seigneury of Montpellier in Languedoc, and Catalan lands east of the Pyrenees, including Roussillon and Cerdagne. Peter's opposition to his brother's inheritance led to a period of war and uncertainty that ended in 1298 with an agreement in which James II retook the Kingdom of Mallorca but pledged fealty to the king of Aragon. The Kingdom of Mallorca was short-lived, however. In 1343 King Peter IV of Aragon invaded and installed a governor who ruled on his behalf. In 1479, under the "Catholic Monarchs" King Ferdinand II of Aragon and Queen Isabella I of Castile, the dynastic union of Spain was achieved, although the two kingdoms remained distinct until the early eighteenth century.

Even under Muslim rule, the island of Mallorca was a crucial transit point for Catalan and Italian merchants. This economic integration into Mediterranean commercial networks may have undermined Mallorca's viability as a political entity independent from the Crown of Aragon, but it also made the island a rich center for art and architecture. In its primary city, Palma de Mallorca, wealthy merchants joined the ranks of the aristocracy as patrons of art and architecture. This is reflected in the large number of *casas señoriales* constructed in fifteenth- and sixteenth-century Palma. These grand homes, found across the major Catalan cities of the Crown of Aragon, often united smaller preexisting structures around a new central courtyard adorned with richly decorated architectural elements, including a stairway and gallery (see fig. 1).[3] This arrangement is quite common in Islamic architecture—it provides air circulation and shade in hot climates—and its popularity in Mallorca speaks to the enduring influence of Islamic architectural modalities even as patrons and architects sought to declare a new Christian identity by embracing European stylistic languages.[4] In the fifteenth century Mallorcan architecture employed a Gothic vocabulary found throughout Catalan-speaking lands; the influence of Italian architecture became more pronounced in the sixteenth century.

While several *casas señoriales* stand in Palma to this day, only vestiges of their fifteenth- and sixteenth-century decoration survive.[5] Elaborated over the course of centuries by successive generations, these homes often included a mixture of different styles. In the seventeenth and eighteenth centuries, shifting tastes caused many owners to remove earlier ornate sculptural work. In the late nineteenth and early twentieth centuries, a growing international market for this architectural sculpture incentivized property owners and dealers to dismantle and sell remaining elements; urbanization projects, such as the creation of new thoroughfares, also led to the destruction of historic homes. Although grand stairways were the central organizing feature of fifteenth-century patios in *casas señoriales*, only one survives in Palma: that of Can Oleo, now part of the Universitat de les Illes Balears, which boasts panels adorned with sculpted tracery rosettes {6}. Better preserved are sixteenth-century stairways with iron railings that lead to second-floor galleries, but these are generally

{6}
Stairway of Can Oleo, Carrer de l'Almudaina, 4, Palma de Mallorca, Spain

restrained in their ornament. For the most part, nineteenth- and early twentieth-century photographs, drawings, and descriptive texts composed by visitors to Mallorca entranced by these stately homes offer the best insight into this architectural typology and its evolution.[6]

Princeton's Stairway and Gallery

The stairway and gallery elements donated to the Museum by Baroness Cassel van Doorn can now be added to the small corpus of surviving records of this distinctive form of residential architecture. Made up of more than one hundred pieces of limestone, Princeton's ensemble is composed of three primary architectural features, all of which are adorned with intricate sculptural decoration: (1) eight panels from a stairway, each featuring a tracery rosette flanked by banderoles and topped by a small object resembling spooled thread or a small wind instrument; (2) four columns, bases, and capitals and two half columns, bases, and capitals; (3) eighteen sections of balusters joined together to form multiple balustrades {7} (see also pp. 72–86). Additional accompanying stone elements include newel posts and railings for the stairway and balustrades, as well as a charming fantastical creature that sits atop a newel post.

The patio elements were long understood by the Museum to come from a single Spanish residence built in 1549, the date carved into a cartouche on one of the column bases (see p. 85). This was not an unreasonable assumption: they had been installed as a single, unified composition at the baroness's home, and the drawings and blueprints that accompanied her gift to the Museum further suggested this understanding. Stylistic examination conducted during their conservation treatment called this notion into question, however. The sculptural ornamentation of Princeton's stairway finds direct comparisons in late fifteenth- and early sixteenth-century Mallorcan stairways, while the balustrades and columns of the gallery reflect mid-sixteenth-century stylistic developments across the island that adapt Italian models. While *casas señoriales* often contained a mixture of sculptural and architectural styles reflecting different moments of intervention and expansion, documentary evidence presented in the essays that follow reveals that, in the case of the Princeton ensemble, the stairway and gallery originated from at least two different *casas señoriales* in Palma: The stairway was likely once installed in a residence on Carrer de l'Aigua, and the balustrades and columns were once part of the galleries of Can Ayamans on Carrer d'en Morei.

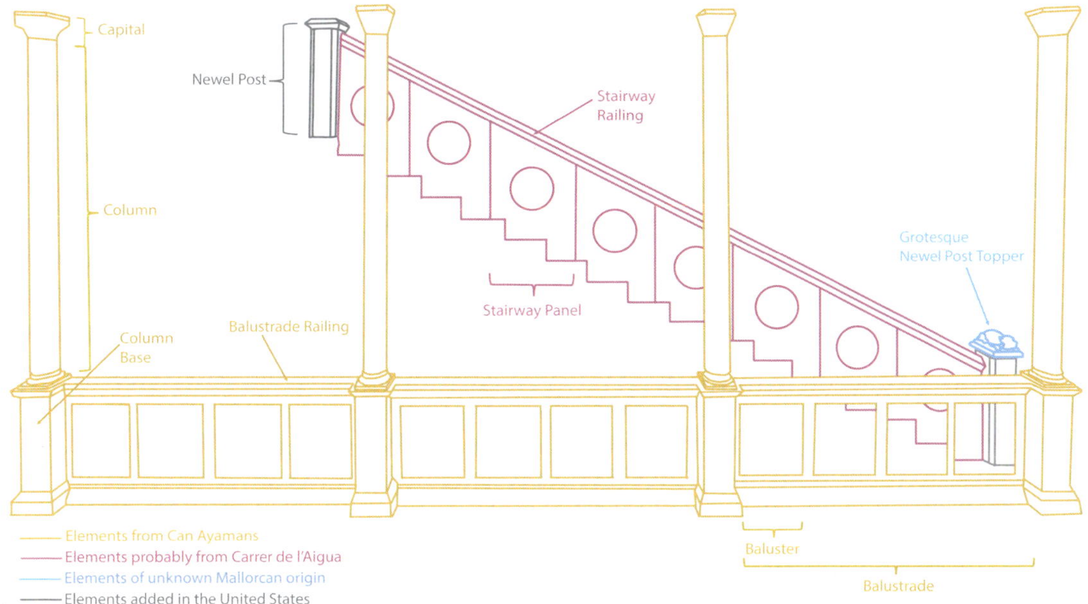

{7}
Elements composing the Mallorcan stairway and gallery, as installed in the Princeton University Art Museum, 2025. Additional gallery elements were not included in the 2025 installation

Princeton's stairway stands apart from other Mallorcan examples in its inscribed banderoles, but its rosettes featuring a variety of tracery patterns find a clear formal parallel in the stairway of Can Oleo (see fig. 6). The early twentieth-century architect and art dealer Arthur Byne recognized this similarity as well: He illustrated sections of both stairways on a single page in *Majorcan Houses and Gardens*, a 1928 publication that he coauthored with his wife, Mildred Stapley Byne {8}.[7] Of the three panels from the "Calle del Agua" (the Castilian name for Carrer de l'Aigua) that Byne depicts, only the central one is a near-exact match to a panel in Princeton's collections. The first and third are similar to ones at Princeton, however, and Byne's architectural drawings frequently approximate rather than accurately document his subjects.

In comparison to the stairway, the balustrades and columns from Can Ayamans that make up Princeton's gallery elements are extraordinarily well documented. Can Ayamans, which still stands today, was among the most significant *casas señoriales* in Palma and was illustrated and photographed several times in the nineteenth century (see figs. 1, 47–51).[8] Parts of the structure date to the thirteenth century, when it was owned by the Morei family, but Felip Fuster transformed the residence after purchasing it in 1531 and adorned two patios with decorative stonework.[9] It is possible that Fuster

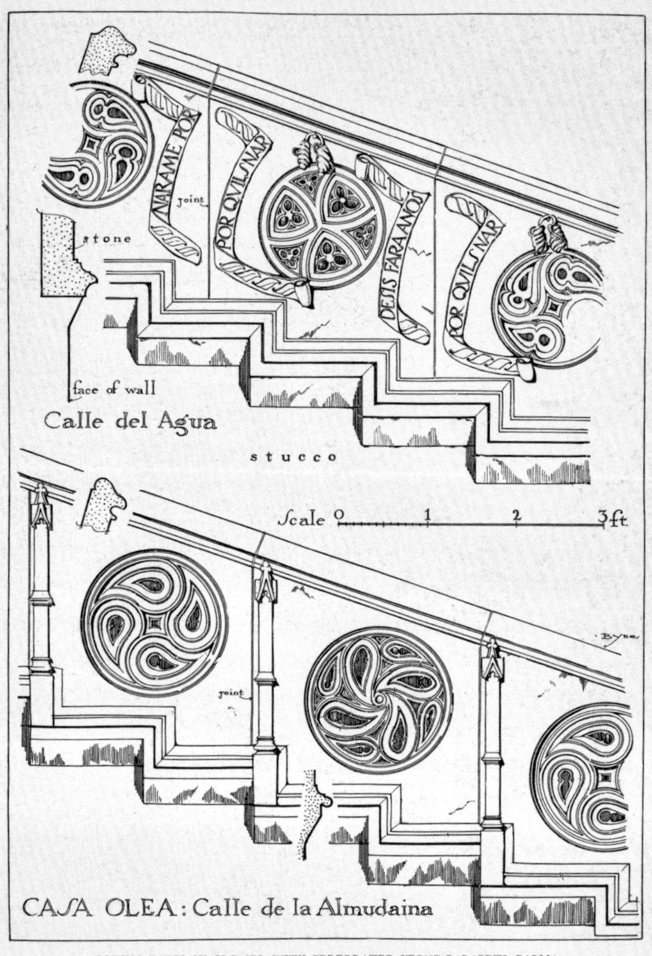
MAJORCAN HOUSES AND GARDENS

PLATE 160

GOTHIC PATIO STAIRCASES, WITH PERFORATED STONE PARAPETS, PALMA

In the Gothic period the stair was attached to the patio wall and left uncovered; subsequently it was set back within the house

{8}
Arthur Byne, illustrations of stairways from a house on the Calle del Agua and Casa Olea [Can Oleo], in Arthur Byne and Mildred Stapley Byne, *Majorcan Houses and Gardens: A Spanish Island in the Mediterranean* (W. Helburn, 1928)

commissioned the sculptor Joan de Salas, active in Mallorca between 1529 and 1536, to execute this plan.[10] Indeed, the carved decoration on Princeton's columns and balustrades bears a strong resemblance to the ornamental reliefs, figures, and masks that Salas carved for one of his documented commissions, the choir portal of the Cathedral of Mallorca {9}. The cartouche on the column base inscribed with the year 1549 postdates Salas's death in 1538; this date might correspond to another event in the house's history, however, or it might mark the completion of the entire renovation project, perhaps by members of Salas's workshop. Despite its status as one of the finest *casas señoriales* in Mallorca, Can Ayamans had been stripped of its sculpted gallery elements by the late nineteenth century. By 1925 they were in the possession of the Mallorcan dealer Josep Costa Ferrer (also known as Picarol), who commissioned a Mallorcan sculptor, Miguel Sacanell, to restore them.[11]

A New Assemblage

In the late 1920s Princeton's stairway and gallery were joined together and marketed as a single ensemble from a grand Mallorcan residence.[12] The essays in this volume detail how this came to be, the people involved in bringing these elements from Palma to Princeton, and the physical changes these stones underwent, which forever transformed them.

The story of Princeton's Mallorcan patio elements is remarkable for the wealth of documentation that survives regarding their creation, restoration, purchase, export, and integration into new settings in the United States. The extraordinary volume and diversity of materials related to the creation of this hybrid ensemble—from photographs and sketches to sales records and letters—offer an unusually rich opportunity to reconstruct its story. Nonetheless, the ensemble's creation and export to the United States are not without precedent or context. In the early twentieth century—a time of intense American fascination with Spanish art and culture—many collectors purchased Spanish architectural elements and even entire structures to incorporate into residences and museums.[13] Around 1913, for example, the German-born banker George Blumenthal acquired the spectacular early sixteenth-century marble patio from the Castle of Vélez Blanco in Almería, Spain.[14] He incorporated the stones into the central hall of his New York City mansion on Seventieth Street and Park Avenue along with a wide array of European art and architectural elements {10}. Upon his death in 1941, he bequeathed his home and its contents to

{9}
Joan de Salas (born Spain; died 1538; active 16th century), Choir portal, Cathedral of Mallorca, Palma, early 16th century

{10}
Patio from the Castle of Vélez Blanco, Almería, Spain, 1506–15; installed in the home of George and Florence Blumenthal, 50 East Seventieth Street, New York, NY, 1920s. The Metropolitan Museum of Art, New York. Thomas J. Watson Library

the Metropolitan Museum of Art. After years of planning, in 1963 and 1964—at the precise moment that Princeton was preparing to install the Mallorcan stairway and gallery—the Vélez Blanco patio was reassembled as the central feature of a new wing built to house the Thomas J. Watson Library at the Met {11}.[15]

Shortly before the patio opened to the public, Olga Raggio, associate research curator of Western European arts, articulated the Met's goal to "reproduce as faithfully as possible its original aspect," a task complicated by the lack of thorough photographic documentation of the patio and one that required her to travel to the original site in Spain to take measurements and photographs. Even with this diligent research, many changes to the patio were made to accommodate the space available at the Met, such as the orientation of the stairway and the placement of a doorway. New elements were also introduced to complete the ensemble, including Sevillian ceiling tiles and an Italian balcony and portal.[16] As Raggio acknowledged in internal correspondence, the project "would seem to be more correctly described as a re-adaptation of the Vélez architectural elements rather than as a strict architectural reconstruction.... Seen as a gallery, simply suggestive of a Spanish Renaissance *Patio* ... [it] appears as a harmonious and attractive area."[17]

As the case of the Vélez Blanco patio makes clear, with every transfer in ownership—and accompanying acts of dismantling and reassembling—the identity of architectural elements unmoored from their original contexts becomes increasingly obscured. When the Mallorcan stairway and gallery came to Princeton, significantly less was known about them than was known about the Vélez Blanco patio, making it impossible for the Museum to consider emulating the Met's example of sending a representative to Spain to measure or photograph an original site. Instead the elements were arranged to best fit the space available in the new medieval gallery and provide a historically inflected atmosphere in which to appreciate the Museum's medieval collections.

The recovery of the story of the Mallorcan stairway and gallery presented in the two essays that follow reveals that there was in fact no single original context for the elements before the 1920s, making the goal of a faithful reconstruction unattainable. This is often the case for European architectural fragments that were exported to the United States in the early twentieth century. Once integrated into museum galleries as representatives of architectural types, however, they frequently impart a visual coherence that implies an impossible

{11}
Patio from the Castle of Vélez Blanco, Almería, Spain, 1506–15. The Metropolitan Museum of Art, New York. Bequest of George Blumenthal, 1941 (41.190.482)

level of historical authenticity. While the Mallorcan stairway and gallery were previously displayed in this manner at Princeton, their new installation—an undertaking that involved the efforts of curators, conservators, art handlers, riggers, masons, designers, structural engineers, and other specialists—presents the elements as two fragments united by a shared past, making visible a history previously unknown to the Museum and inviting visitors to appreciate this monumental ensemble's grandeur.

ALEXANDRA LETVIN

Reimagining a Mallorcan Patio: A Winding Journey from Palma to Princeton

The Mallorcan stairway and gallery's journey from Palma to Princeton was shaped by a succession of individuals throughout the twentieth century who transformed architectural elements from at least two *casas señoriales* (stately or noble residences) into the ensemble now on view in the Entrance Hall of the Princeton University Art Museum. When they arrived at the Museum in 1955, the stairway and gallery were associated with only two names: the art dealer Arthur Byne and Baroness Cassel van Doorn. With little known about either, the Museum long assumed that the baroness had purchased the stairway and gallery directly from Byne. Investigating the lives of these two figures and their partners unearths a much richer story about the Mallorcan patio elements, however, revealing a network of dealers and collectors in Europe and the United States who interpreted and reinterpreted these architectural fragments. The resulting trans-atlantic narrative illuminates broader trends in art collecting between Europe and the United States and intersects with some of the most significant cultural property debates of the twentieth century.

Arthur Byne (1884–1935) and Mildred Stapley Byne (1875–1941)

Arthur Byne was an American architect who became an art dealer in the 1920s {12}. Based in Spain, he supplied wealthy American clients and museums with Spanish art, decorative arts, architectural

{12}
Arthur Byne, undated photograph. California Polytechnic State University, San Luis Obispo. Special Collections and Archives, Julia Morgan Papers

{13}
Christina Morton (1891–1957), *Mildred Stapley Byne*, ca. 1931. Oil on canvas. Photographed by Peter A. Juley & Son. Smithsonian American Art Museum, Washington, DC. Juley & Son Collection, Photograph Study Collection (J0099237)

elements, and at times even entire buildings. With his wife and business partner, Mildred Stapley Byne {13}, he published significant texts on Spanish art and architecture that encouraged a growing appreciation for Spanish culture. As an art dealer, however, he frequently engaged in activities that today would be considered unethical and in many cases illegal, earning him and Stapley the distinction of being described recently as "the greatest plunderers of Spanish art of the twentieth century."[1]

Born Arthur Gustave Bein on September 25, 1884, in Newark, New Jersey, Byne—who anglicized the spelling of his last name in 1911—grew up in New Haven, Connecticut.[2] He trained as an architect at the University of Pennsylvania and then continued his studies for two years at the American Academy in Rome. In 1908 he moved to New York and became a designer for the architectural firm Howells & Stokes.[3] A gifted draftsman and watercolorist, he won a silver medal for one of his watercolors at the 1915 Panama-Pacific International Exposition in San Francisco and illustrated several covers of *The Architectural Record* {14} {15}.

In 1910 Byne married Mildred Stapley, a portrait painter who had studied in Paris and New York. She had developed a fascination with Spain after attending, as "a young girl," a lecture on El Greco given by the American painter William Merritt Chase (1849–1916).[4] She recalled: "I shall never forget that portrait of a Spaniard, bronzed,

{14}
Arthur Byne, *Cathedral of Segovia*, watercolor illustration for the cover of *The Architectural Record*, August 1917

{15}
Arthur Byne, *Santiago Cathedral*, watercolor illustration for the cover of *The Architectural Record*, September 1917

vivid, bold and painted with a daring disregard of the conventions of academic art. It set my imagination on fire. As I looked at it and listened to Chase discuss 'El Greco,' I determined to study the Spanish masters in their native land." An avid traveler, she soon went to Spain with her mother because she "was eager to paint and sketch there."[5]

Stapley introduced Byne to Spain; they traveled there together shortly after their wedding. Years later she described the impetus for that trip:

> On marrying, [I] suggested to my husband, architect by profession, that Spain contained a wealth of architecture and minor art practically unknown to American architects, so here we came to look over the field and found it even richer than we suspected. Particularly struck by the grandeur and monumentality of Spanish ironwork as found in the cathedrals we began to study it with enthusiasm, photographing, measuring, drawing, and searching for information on the subject, printed or unprinted. It happened that the former sort did not exist, for Spain has been very slow to make known her artistic treasures even to her own people.[6]

Stapley's suggestion that the couple travel to Spain was perhaps designed to build on and take advantage of the voracious appetite among Americans for Spanish culture that took root in the 1890s and continued until approximately 1930. Joining this fervor—known as the Spanish Craze or Spanish Fever—were artists such as Chase and John Singer Sargent, as well as several collectors who developed a newfound interest in purchasing Spanish art and emulating Spanish architecture.[7] For example, in addition to acquiring important Spanish pictures beginning in the late 1890s, Isabella Stewart Gardner designed in 1914 a "Spanish Cloister" {16} and adjacent chapel for her Venetian-style residence and museum in Boston, combining decorative and architectural elements from Spain, Mexico, Italy, Egypt, Iran, and Turkey to provide an atmospheric—if factitious and fantastical—setting for Sargent's celebrated painting of a flamenco dancer, *El Jaleo* (1882).[8] In contrast to this hybrid approach, in 1910 the German-born banker George Blumenthal acquired a spectacular example of early sixteenth-century Spanish architecture—the patio from the Castle of Vélez Blanco—that he incorporated into the central hall of his New York mansion with somewhat greater attention to historical accuracy (see fig. 10).[9]

Byne took countless photographs during the couple's trip to Spain that may have served as his introduction to one of the great promoters of Spanish art and culture in the United States, Archer Milton Huntington (1870–1955). The son of a wealthy railroad and

{16}
The Spanish Cloister, Isabella Stewart Gardner Museum, Boston

shipbuilding magnate, Huntington developed a passion for Spain that led him, in 1904, to found the Hispanic Society of America in New York, a public library and museum with a mission to advance "the study of the Spanish and Portuguese languages, literature and history."[10] In December 1913 Byne wrote to Huntington asking for a meeting to discuss publishing a book on sixteenth-century Spanish art and noted that his friend and employer, Phelps Stokes, had already written to Huntington about Byne's photographs of Spain.[11] This meeting appears to have gone well: In 1914 Huntington named Byne and Stapley corresponding members of the Hispanic Society, and in 1916 they became the society's first curators of architecture and the allied arts, a position that primarily entailed documenting architectural sites in Spain. Between 1915 and 1918 Huntington financed four trips for the duo to travel throughout the country and photograph monuments, many of which were little known and in remote locations. Some of their approximately twelve hundred photographs were exhibited at the Hispanic Society in 1917, and all were available for consultation in the institution's library, including a 1915 image of the stairway from the patio of Can Oleo in Palma de Mallorca {17}.[12]

The Bynes' affiliation with the Hispanic Society gave them unprecedented access to sites throughout Spain, including private collections. They advertised these connections in eight books on Spanish art and architecture for which Stapley wrote the text and Byne contributed photographs and drawings.[13] In the preface to one of their early publications, *Spanish Architecture of the Sixteenth Century*, Byne and Stapley situate themselves within the lineage of foundational eighteenth- and nineteenth-century Spanish art historians such as Antonio Ponz (1725–1792) and Juan Agustín Ceán Bermúdez (1749–1829), elevating the status of their books to seminal reference texts.[14] A common refrain in their publications and correspondence is that their work is intended to reveal the treasures of Spain not only to an international audience but also to a Spanish one. In 1919, for example, they wrote to Huntington that some in Spain might "feel ill-used because the Yanquis have brought to light what they themselves have allowed to lie in darkness for centuries."[15] This paternalistic tone also appears throughout their correspondence as dealers, often serving as a justification and guiding philosophy for their actions.

Their books were positively received in the United States and Spain. In 1922 a Spanish journalist wrote: "How can Spain pay a fitting tribute to the authors of these works, one that will indicate the gratitude the nation feels to Mr. and Mrs. Byne, a pair of wonderful,

{17}
Arthur Byne, *Palma de Mallorca: Casa Oleo, Patio Stair,* 16th century. Photograph from the 1915 Byne expedition, no. 557. Hispanic Society Museum & Library, New York

adorable Americans who have honored before the whole world romantic Spain?"[16] They also found enthusiastic readers in the United States. Reviewing *Provincial Houses in Spain* in *The Architectural Record*, one critic remarked, "The growth of interest in Spanish architecture in this country is closely associated with their books, already considerable in number, all important and authoritative, all useful for an architect's library."[17]

In practice, these publications also functioned as inspiration and sometimes sales catalogs for the many wealthy American collectors who were growing increasingly captivated by Spanish culture. To avoid depleting Spain of its artistic riches, Huntington maintained a policy of acquiring only significant Spanish art that had already been exported from the country.[18] Byne and Stapley's developing interest in and preference for selling art directly from Spain led to growing tensions with him. In 1918 the Hispanic Society ended the couple's contract as curators but commissioned them to prepare publications on Spanish art and architecture. Huntington came to suspect, however, that Byne and Stapley were using their time in Spain and affiliation with the Hispanic Society to further their personal ambitions and that they were breaking the terms of their contract by engaging in private research during travel funded by the society. In 1919 he wrote of the pair: "They have limitations which may be hard to conquer. Vanity is their danger," alluding perhaps to their growing interest in Spain's social hierarchy and accessing private collections.[19] Finally, in 1921, Byne and Stapley requested a formal separation from the Hispanic Society. Byne asked for the return of all his drawings and photographic negatives—including those he had made as a representative of the society—and the trustees agreed, provided the society could retain copies of the photographs.

William Randolph Hearst (1863–1951), Julia Morgan (1872–1957), and La Cuesta Encantada

While Byne and Stapley were making this career transition, Stapley had been corresponding with an old friend from Paris, Julia Morgan. In 1902 Morgan became the first woman to graduate with a certificate from the architecture program of the École des Beaux-Arts in Paris; in 1904 she became the first woman licensed to practice architecture in California and opened her own firm in her native San Francisco.[20] Byne and Stapley's photographs of Spain had attracted her attention as early as 1914, when she wrote to Stapley about an unnamed "friend" interested in purchasing a selection of them. Stapley sent Morgan

135 plates of primarily "Renaissance, Romanesque and Gothic" architecture, explaining: "It w[oul]d be impossible to buy a similar collection in Spain or out of it, the Spanish having paid no attention to photographing their monuments, except the best known & most accessible. You will see that these are gathered from remote places seldom visited even by architects."[21] Only Stapley's letters to Morgan are preserved from this exchange, but Morgan or her friend deemed the couple's asking price—$2 a photograph, $175 for 100, or $300 for 175—too high, and she returned them.

The next surviving correspondence between Stapley and Morgan dates seven years later, to September 1921. Morgan asked Stapley for detail photographs from a Byne-Stapley publication and told her of an exciting new project she was undertaking for the newspaper magnate William Randolph Hearst, perhaps the "friend" mentioned in her earlier correspondence {18}. Hearst's flamboyant personality and the breathtaking pace and volume of his art acquisitions were both legendary and lampooned in his lifetime. After convincing his father—an extremely successful prospector—to give him control of *The San Francisco Examiner* at age twenty-four, Hearst built a media empire. He lived lavishly, conceiving and furnishing six palatial residences in California, New York, and Wales. He purchased not only art to decorate these homes but also countless historical architectural

{18}
William Randolph Hearst with Julia Morgan during the construction of Hearst Castle, 1926

{19}
San Simeon Aerial View, 1931. California Polytechnic State University, San Luis Obispo. Special Collections and Archives, Julia Morgan Papers

elements and even entire buildings to incorporate into them. Hearst's collecting—which ranged from ancient Greek vases to old master paintings, from tapestries to arms and armor, and from Georgian silver to Spanish ceilings—has been studied by numerous scholars who have offered various interpretations for his seemingly insatiable appetite for art, including megalomania and a commitment to designing multiple extravagant residences in different styles.[22]

Morgan described their current project to Stapley: "We are building for him a sort of village on a mountain-top overlooking the sea and ranges and ranges of mountains, miles from any railway, and housing incidentally, his collections as well as his family."[23] This would become La Cuesta Encantada (the enchanted hill) in San Simeon, California, popularly known as Hearst Castle {19}. Hearst had first begun discussing the site—a sixteen-hundred-foot-high peak on land his family owned on California's Central Coast—with Morgan in 1919. He initially intended to build a smaller structure, possibly a Craftsman-style bungalow, but the project quickly expanded.[24] By 1947, when Hearst's declining health compelled him to leave San Simeon, the estate included the 68,500-square-foot Casa Grande as well as three guesthouses and two swimming pools.

Sensing an opportunity, Stapley responded to Morgan's letter promptly, asking—perhaps with a note of irony—if Morgan might know of anyone interested in acquiring Spanish art:

> Our opportunities for disposing of good old private collections were so numerous that it seemed a pity not to take advantage of them, so we have become antiquaries.... Many things are brought to our attention to be quietly sold that would never reach the ordinary dealer, and our good judgment and fair dealing stand high both with the seller and the purchaser. Should you know of anyone in S.F. [San Francisco] who wants genuine old Spanish articles sent direct, anything from a bride's chest of old linens to the contents of a whole cast castillo [*sic*], will you be good enough to mention us?[25]

Morgan passed this along to Hearst, noting to Stapley: "Your books are as a gospel to him. I hope it will bring results."[26] Indeed, a few weeks later Hearst instructed Morgan to "correspond with the lady and ask her to act as agent for us. We will want a tremendous lot of stuff... and probably we could do much better from her than from the average antiquary."[27] Byne assured Morgan: "No one in all Spain is in touch with salable treasures to the extent that we are, and... we ask less profit on any transaction than the rapacious professional antiquarians."[28] From this point forward, Byne took over most correspondence with Morgan and Hearst regarding the sale of art and became Hearst's primary agent in Spain.

Hearst decided to build San Simeon in a Spanish style to honor California's history as a former Spanish colony. His interest in Spain is often associated with the 1898 Spanish-American War, in which his newspapers took an anti-Spanish stance. He had studied Spanish at Harvard University in the 1880s, however, an unusual choice at a time when most Americans studied German or French and one that may have reflected his upbringing in California and interactions with workers of Mexican heritage employed by his father.[29] Hearst had begun acquiring Spanish lusterware by 1899, but two trips to Spain and Portugal in 1905 and 1911 were crucial to his developing interest in Spanish art and architecture, and it was during this time that he made his first documented attempt to purchase a large architectural ensemble from Spain, discussed below.[30] Hearst gravitated toward Spanish art and architecture produced around 1500, rather than Baroque ("over-elaborate"), viceregal ("sometimes too elaborate"),

{20}
"Old Church of Santa María la Mayor, Ronda, Spain," ca. 1892–1930. Published by Keystone View Company. Library of Congress, Washington, DC. Prints and Photographs Division

or California Mission style ("too bare and clumsy").[31] He was particularly drawn to the mixture of styles he saw in the Collegiate Church of Santa María la Mayor in Ronda {20}, which he would later ask Morgan to emulate in her design for the towers of the Casa Grande of San Simeon. Byne and Stapley's *Spanish Architecture of the Sixteenth Century*, which Hearst sent to Morgan in 1919 as she was designing San Simeon, was thus perfectly pitched to his taste.[32]

While Hearst had been interested in and aware of Spanish art for several decades, it was only as the San Simeon project took shape that he embarked on the large-scale collecting of Spanish art and architectural elements, an endeavor facilitated by Byne and Stapley. There were many ups and downs to this business relationship. Hearst's payments frequently came late, requiring Byne on more than one occasion to adopt an admonishing tone. At one point Byne exasperatedly wrote: "To tell the plain truth, Miss Morgan, I cannot do business with Mr. Hearst.... He makes a business (and incidentally considerable gain) of holding people off for years and then settling on his own terms. Now, of course that is all right when you are dealing with [major dealers] Duveen or Seligmann because their prices cover all eventualities. But I quoted prices to Mr. Hearst for one quarter of what he would have to pay in either New York or Paris, but of course on a strictly cash basis."[33]

Despite these disagreements, in the fourteen years that they worked together, Hearst acquired from Byne and Stapley countless works, from tiles to dozens of ceilings to two entire cloisters, now assembled in much-altered states in Florida and California {21} {22}. To transact at such a scale, they developed an efficient system of communicating across the Atlantic: Byne would send photographs in letters and assign each object an abbreviated name; Hearst or Morgan would respond via telegram. Sometimes Hearst would tell Byne to purchase a specific item; at other times he would deposit a lump sum in an account and tell Byne to spend it down. Some objects were shipped directly to California and promptly integrated into the buildings at San Simeon; others were sent to a five-story warehouse in the Bronx, New York, owned by the International Studio Art Corporation, a Hearst Corporation subsidiary created in the early 1920s to receive, inventory, store, and ship Hearst's growing number of acquisitions.[34]

{21}
Cloister of the Monastery of Saint Bernard de Clairvaux, 12th century; built in Sacramenia (Segovia), Spain; purchased by William Randolph Hearst via Arthur Byne, 1925; rebuilt in the 1950s in North Miami Beach, Florida

{22}
Stones from the Monastery of Santa María de Óliva, 12th century; built near Trillo (Guadalajara), Spain; purchased by William Randolph Hearst via Arthur Byne, 1931; partially rebuilt and reimagined in the 2000s in Vina, California, as the Chapter House for the Abbey of New Clairvaux

Navigating Spanish Cultural Patrimony Laws

One impediment to Byne's success and Hearst's collecting ambitions was a developing concept of and legal framework for cultural patrimony in Spain. The early twentieth century was a time of significant political upheaval in the country, as it transitioned from a monarchy under King Alfonso XIII (r. 1902–31)—which included a period of dictatorship under General Miguel Primo de Rivera (1923–30)—to a form of democratic government under the Second Spanish Republic (1931–39), and finally to the dictatorship of General Francisco Franco (1936–75) following the devastating Spanish Civil War (1936–39). With varying degrees of success, each of these governments introduced legislation intended to regulate the international trade of Spanish art and architecture, prompted in part by the activities of dealers like Byne.

The first Spanish laws governing the export of art date to the late eighteenth century, but these did not apply to property of the Catholic Church and were not consistently enforced, particularly when agents such as Byne resorted to "subsidiary commissions of a legal and illegal nature"—in other words, bribes.[35] Similarly, the first national

monument—León Cathedral—was declared in 1844, but a systematic policy regarding such designations was not formalized until almost a century later.[36] Following World War I, during which Spain remained neutral, a period of economic growth led to the dismantling or demolition of many historic buildings to make way for new construction, creating employment within Spain and lucrative sales opportunities for dealers.[37] It was only in the late 1920s and early 1930s that more coherent policies regarding the export of art began to take shape.[38] This initially afforded Byne a great deal of latitude, provided he kept his exploits quiet and avoided the negative press coverage that accompanied many failed exportation attempts.

In 1904, for example, news of the purchase and export of the patio of Vélez Blanco to Paris, where it would later be acquired by Blumenthal (see figs. 10, 11), led to public outcry in Spain and condemnations of the government's disregard for national patrimony and complicity in an act of spoliation.[39] Hearst experienced a similar reaction in 1910, when he attempted to dismantle and export a mid-fifteenth-century patio from the Casa Miranda in Burgos that the city had declined to purchase {23}.[40] After he paid a deposit of $16,000 (approximately $515,000 in 2024), news of his acquisition in progress led to widespread protest in Spain and a temporary injunction on the patio's removal.[41] The scandal reached the American press, prompting *The New York Times* to opine: "The apprehension of Burgos is not unjustifiable. But these reawakened foreign folk ought to be grateful to the American collectors, or the shrewd, speculative dealers who buy things for them, for stirring up their pride."[42] With the support of US Ambassador Joseph Willard, Hearst's case was brought to Spain's supreme court, which in June 1915 ruled in favor of his right to purchase the patio. King Alfonso XIII then declared the patio a national monument, blocking its dismantling and export. This blow continued to fester for years; in 1919 Hearst wrote to Morgan: "By the way I own [that patio] but cannot get it out of Spain."[43]

Byne would later use this incident to remind Morgan of his own discretion in successfully exporting art from Spain. In 1925 he embarked on the complex, lengthy, and legally dubious process of dismantling the cloister of the Cistercian Monastery of Saint Bernard de Clairvaux in Sacramenia (Segovia) for Hearst (see fig. 21). Hearst intended the cloister for an unrealized museum at the University of California, Berkeley, and Byne compared the sale to the Metropolitan Museum of Art's recent acquisition of a cloister assembled by George Grey Barnard—an American sculptor, collector, and dealer—which

{23}
Genaro Pérez Villaamil, "Patio de la Casa Miranda en Burgos," lithograph in Genaro Pérez Villaamil and Patricio de la Escosura, *España artística y monumental*, vol. 2 (Paris, 1844)

would form the core of the Met Cloisters.[44] As the project progressed, Byne commented to Morgan, seemingly (but improbably) unaware of Hearst's stake in the Burgos matter: "Buying these old buildings is not quite as easy as Mr. Hearst imagines. Our American Embassador [*sic*] to Spain (who is not conspicuous for doing the tactful thing) tried to secure the famous Casa de Miranda of Burgos recently (I fancy for Mr. Hearst). Publicity in purchases of important works of art is always most disastrous and when no less a person that [*sic*] the American Embassador to Spain tries to buy a famous palace by putting the announcement in the press it forever spoilt any chances there were to ship the Miranda out of Spain."[45]

Growing governmental oversight and regulation of the trade and export of art in the late 1920s put increasing pressure on Byne. In 1926 Primo de Rivera granted the Royal Academy of Fine Arts and the Royal Academy of History the authority to block the export of objects. In June 1931 the Second Republic formalized a far-reaching policy regarding the declaration of monuments as national artistic treasures that effectively prevented private citizens and the Church from selling objects deemed to be of national interest. The decree included 755 newly protected sites, dramatically and immediately increasing the number of national monuments from 362 to 1,117.[46]

Although Byne continued to operate clandestinely, the situation was volatile and tense. This unpredictability could work in his favor, as Spanish property owners were often eager to sell when they could. But there was no end to his frustrations, with countless purchases in process shut down by the government. In his correspondence with Hearst and Morgan, Byne frequently referred to the shifting landscape regarding the export of works of art, with new obstacles posed by local or national governments, Church officials, the exchange rate, or impending unrest. In July 1931, a month after the Second Republic introduced its new policy, he summarized concisely: "[The] Minister of Belles Artes [fine arts] seems determined to make a National Monument out of every sand heap.... Conditions in the country are very uncertain and contradictory laws are being turned out by the bushel every day."[47]

Often Byne tried to use Spain's instability to encourage his client to move forward with a purchase on which he was wavering. Sometimes, it seems, Hearst could be persuaded; at other times, however, he appears not to have been easily manipulated by these pressure campaigns. Hearst also seems to have had some sympathy for Spain's perspective; in 1934 he remarked, "Spain ought to be like

Italy and keep the important things in the important places because that is what brings the tourists and the tourists are about all that is profitable."[48]

The Mallorcan Stairway and Gallery

As Hearst's purchase of the Sacramenia cloister approached completion, Morgan instructed Byne to find a second cloister that would be incorporated into the design of a new house in Los Angeles.[49] In August 1925 she wrote:

> In addition to the San Simeon estate, Mr. Hearst is to build a house proper, (single house) in Los Angeles.—Hence the call for the second cloister. He wants you, if interested, to find him a fine, even celebrated house that could be taken apart and rebuilt here, (with changes of course) or a patio from one house and the doors, trim, cornice, etc. from another—or a fine cloister and a house exterior, etc. (as your imagination can make it). He would pay the price necessary to obtain something really fine. You could buy the properties maybe and if necessary to have a special permit to get [them] out of Spain, perhaps we could help from this end.[50]

As Morgan made clear, Hearst's interest was less in historical authenticity than in achieving a desired aesthetic effect. A week later she continued: "But he does want for himself something really very fine, gothique [*sic*], transitional, or Renaissance and I am sure if you would find the something the question of expense would not enter. I imagine you are laughing—you and Mildred—when you get this request, but Mr. Hearst announced last night 'You know we sent Mr. Byne a perfectly good list of pictures of possible looking patios and cloisters and surely some of these Signors, Dukes, etc are hard enough up to part with *one* of them.'"[51]

In the coming months, Byne proposed patios and cloisters from León, Úbeda, Peñaranda, and Cádiz, all of which fell flat with Hearst. Weighing their aesthetic qualities, in December 1925 Hearst remarked to Morgan: "I think Mr. Byne had better keep hunting. I am sure there are many places that are better, but, of course, the difficulty is in getting good ones out of Spain."[52] As their back-and-forth continued, it became clear that Hearst envisioned not a cloister from a religious building but rather a patio from a noble residence. Morgan offered further insight in March 1926: "If I catch his idea correctly he would

copied for Mr Hearst April 13, 1929

Majorca Pair

Arthur Byne
Paseo de la Castellana, 19
Madrid

S.7
Recd, April 9, 1929

File

March 25th,
1 9 2 9

Miss Julia Morgan,
Merchants Exchange,
San Francisco

Dear Miss Morgan;

I am writing this letter enroute to Madrid from the Island of Majorca where I have been staying a fortnight.

Enclosed find some crude sketches of a remarkably fine late Gothic patio-stair and gallery-two galleries, in fact, and a Gothic window besides.

All this once adorned one of the most famous 16th century palaces of Palma. Forty years ago when the palace was demolished, this stair, the double gallery, and the window were carefully taken down stone by stone and stored away in another palace of the same family. Being now in financial difficulties they have brought the matter to my attention.

The gallery bears the date 1540 and is beautifully carved in Gothic and Renaissance detail (in this part of the world the people clung tenaciously to Gothic well into the 16th century). I have taken some detail photographs which, once developed in Madrid, I will send on later. You will then see that the work is quite exquisite in execution.

On the sketches I have indicated what is included in the price and what is not; many of the purely utilitarian stones, such as the steps, for instance were not saved.

The price is NINE THOUSAND dollars ($9,000.00). In many respects I consider this one of the most important pieces I have brought to your attention and certainly at a bargain price.

not be interested in anything more of the Cistercian period because he does not consider it residential enough. The offered buildings have not enough usable material. His eye is on something more richly ornamented rather than something of value from the purity of its architecture. He is planning, when San Simeon is completed, building a winter residence near Los Angeles and it is for this that he wants the material."[53]

It would be in Mallorca that Byne finally found a patio to suit Hearst's taste: the ensemble now at Princeton. On March 25, 1929, he wrote to Morgan of a "remarkably fine late Gothic patio—stair and gallery—two galleries, in fact, and a Gothic window" that "once adorned one of the most famous 16th century palaces of Palma" {24}. He further explained that the palace was demolished forty years prior, and that these elements were "carefully taken down stone by stone and stored away in another palace of the same family. Being now in financial difficulties they have brought the matter to my attention." He included sketches, now lost, and noted:

> On the sketches I have indicated what is included in the price and what is not; many of the purely utilitarian stones, such as the steps, for instance were not saved. The price is NINE THOUSAND dollars ($9,000.00) [approximately $165,000 in 2024]. In many respects I consider this one of the most important pieces I have brought to your attention and certainly at a bargain price. If this gallery and stair were still in position it would be impossible to purchase it to-day, or at least to remove it. Furthermore the price asked would be double or treble the present asking price. I might also add that being a seaport the carrying charges will be much less than if it were situated in inland Castile.[54]

In the ensuing weeks, Byne sent photographs of the ensemble that are now lost.[55] He then followed up hurriedly on April 14 with a price increase of $500 ($9,000 in 2024) because of "the activities of a local millionaire—a Majorcan who made his fortune in the Argentine and who is building a large house on the Island; hearing of my offer he equaled it compelling me to go higher."[56] It is possible that this was not a fictional character invented to put pressure on Hearst and Morgan but rather the Argentinean Adán Diehl (1895–1959), who was an active arts patron on the island and opened the luxury Hotel Formentor (now part of the Four Seasons chain) on its northern coast in 1929.[57]

{24}
Letter from Arthur Byne to Julia Morgan, March 25, 1929. California Polytechnic State University, San Luis Obispo. Special Collections and Archives, Julia Morgan Papers

In any case, the next day—before she would have received Byne's letter—Morgan sent a telegram confirming Hearst's purchase of the stairway and gallery {25}.[58]

As noted in the introduction to this volume, Byne's assertion that the patio elements came from one of the finest homes in Mallorca is partially correct: the balustrades and columns of the gallery once adorned Can Ayamans, one of the grandest *casas señoriales* in Palma (see figs. 1, 47–51). The residence had undergone major renovations in the sixteenth century, but much of its decoration had been removed by the late nineteenth century.[59] The stairway came from a different house in Palma, however, likely on Carrer de l'Aigua (see fig. 8). It would seem, then, that Byne took seriously Hearst's suggestion that he might combine elements from different houses to compose a suitable patio, even if Byne did not acknowledge the true nature of this assemblage in his sales pitch.

In July, Byne further offered two ceilings related to the Mallorcan stairway and gallery. For the first time in his correspondence about the ensemble, he mentions Can Ayamans as the source for these elements in a letter to Morgan: "Pair of ceilings from the Ayamans Palace in Palma, Majorca; these ceilings covered the two loggias respectively, recently purchased along with the Gothic stair, by Mr. Hearst. The

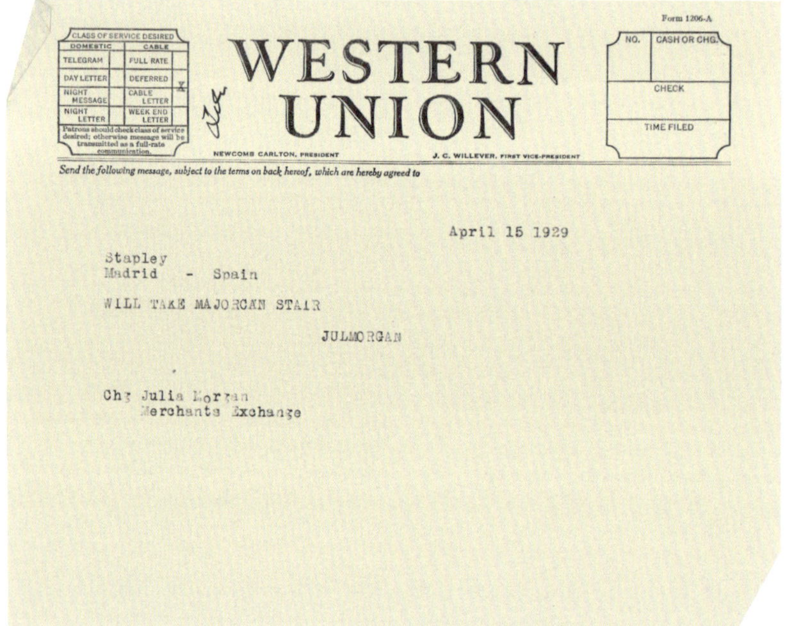

WESTERN UNION

April 15 1929

Stapley
Madrid - Spain

WILL TAKE MAJORCAN STAIR

JULMORGAN

Chg Julia Morgan
Merchants Exchange

{25}
Telegram from Julia Morgan to Arthur Byne, April 15, 1929. California Polytechnic State University, San Luis Obispo. Special Collections and Archives, Julia Morgan Papers

wood is a beautiful Pyreneean [*sic*] red pine, uncolored. The carved detail on the other is extraordinarily fine as indicated in the photographs. An example of the effect produced by this type of Majorcan loggia ceiling is seen on Plate 159, of 'Majorcan Houses and Gardens'" {26}.[60] Not receiving an immediate response, Byne appealed directly to Hearst, writing that the ceilings "would add a great deal to the architectural success of the reconstructed patio."[61] Hearst agreed, and the ceilings were shipped to New York.

At this time Byne sent additional sketches (see figs. 42–45), including an amended version of his March sketch of the gallery and stairway that points out one of the two ceilings that Hearst purchased (see fig. 42).[62] Even in his relatively schematic rendering, it is clear from the banderole and rosettes on the stairway, the cursory sketches of the columns, and the tracery design of the balustrades that the Mallorcan patio complex Hearst purchased is the ensemble now in Princeton. The elements are arranged differently than they were in Princeton's 1965 installation, however, and perhaps differently than Byne first suggested to Hearst and Morgan, as his drawing notes: "Revised for stair showing its original form."[63]

The stairway and gallery were shipped to Hearst's Bronx warehouse and were registered in an album titled "Staircases and Apportenances [*sic*]: Miscellaneous Countries," under the heading "The Majorcan patio and staircase, Spanish, XVI Century" with a purchase date of September 19, 1929.[64] The elements were assigned the inventory number "S/B Lot #275, Art. #1 to 65," which also appears on the reverse of photographs of the drawings now in the Princeton University Art Museum's curatorial files. These once unidentifiable pages in the Museum's records appear to be those from the International Studio Art Corporation's inventory album documenting Hearst's collection.[65]

Mallorcan Allies

The purchase and successful export of the stairway, gallery, and ceilings depended on several factors. Byne acknowledges one—the volatile political situation—explicitly, writing to Morgan:

> Don't think these several fine things have been rounded up in a jiffy; they have been under my wing for years during which time it has been a constant struggle to bring the owners to reason in regard to a practical price. Only the present-day political upheaval in Spain has made it possible to loosen and secure these important features. This same situation will

{26}
Arthur Byne, "Gallery of the Consulado, Palma, 17th Century," photograph in Arthur Byne and Mildred Stapley Byne, *Majorcan Houses and Gardens*, 1928

> assist me to secure two or three other things of importance which are still in the balance and cannot yet be spoken of. Also, another advantage to you is, that the precarious situation of the Spanish government and the consequent depreciation in the value of the peseta has made it possible to secure these objects at a much lower price than before.[66]

Also crucial to the acquisition of the Mallorcan patio elements, however, were Byne and Stapley's carefully cultivated networks. They had been visiting Mallorca since at least 1915, which gave them time to develop relationships with many locals.[67] In 1928 they published *Majorcan Houses and Gardens*, which includes an introductory text by Stapley detailing the island's distinctive architectural features and notes on the histories of fifteen palaces and country houses and their inhabitants, all accompanied by 188 plates featuring Byne's photographs and drawings. The book's prefatory matter acknowledges not only the residents of these buildings for their generosity but also "the painter Don Vicente Furió of Palma, who kindly apprised the authors of and accompanied them to, certain estates of special interest."[68] Indeed, the range of residences they accessed across the island is impressive. As Stapley asserted, "Architecturally [the book] will be a revelation even to those who know the island."[69]

The Bynes were neither the first anglophones nor the first art dealers to discover the riches of Mallorca. The island was a popular destination for nineteenth-century British and American travelers whose written accounts portrayed it as a rustic and remote oasis for those with artistic and literary inclinations.[70] By the late nineteenth century, many *casas señoriales* were being dismantled and their collections liquidated—a product of shifting tastes, urbanization projects, and the growing international market for Spanish art and architecture—making Byne's assertion that the Mallorcan patio elements had been disassembled forty years earlier both probable and not surprising. In the early twentieth century, dealers from Madrid and Barcelona came to Mallorca for short periods and placed announcements in the local newspapers offering to purchase antiques and art from noble families.[71] Byne and Stapley sought to distinguish themselves from these mainland dealers and anglophone tourists by returning to the island again and again and cultivating a network of local dealers, artists, and collectors.

This proved beneficial when, in 1928, Josep Costa Ferrer (1876–1971) founded Galerías Costa, the first permanent center for the art

{27}
Josep Costa Ferrer, undated photograph. Costa Archive

market in Palma {27}. Costa, also known as Picarol, published guides in Spanish and English about the artistic treasures of Mallorca to promote tourism to the island, and he became a key player in the dispersal and sale of *casas señoriales*.[72] Byne and Stapley knew him well: He exhibited Byne's photographs from *Majorcan Houses and Gardens* at his gallery in 1929, and the couple stayed in a home known as El Terreno, owned by a friend of his.[73]

Costa was instrumental in the sale of the Mallorcan patio elements. Though Byne wrote to Morgan that he was approached by the family who owned them, he in fact learned of their availability from Costa. In 1925 Costa had purchased elements from the Can Ayamans patio gallery as a pile of disassembled stones.[74] As detailed in Elena Torok's essay in this volume, Costa hired the Mallorcan sculptor Miguel Sacanell to restore the stones in preparation for a possible sale. Likely in 1929, the fifteenth-century stairway from a house probably on Carrer de l'Aigua was added to the ensemble. It appears that this addition was spearheaded by Byne to create a more "complete" patio that would appeal to Hearst. In any case, after trying and failing to find a Mallorcan buyer, Costa finally sold the Ayamans elements to Byne in 1929. When Byne asked their price, Costa fibbed, claiming that he had paid 5,000 pesetas ($13,183 in 2024) when he had in fact paid

3,000 ($7,910 in 2024), though this inflated figure may have included his outlay for the restoration.[75] Regardless, Costa realized a substantial profit from the sale: he suggested Byne name a price he thought appropriate, and Byne paid him 20,000 pesetas ($52,679 in 2024).[76]

Scholars or Pillagers?

On July 16, 1935, Arthur Byne and Mildred Stapley were driving from Gibraltar to Madrid when they collided with an oncoming truck. Byne was fatally injured; Stapley survived. She stayed in Spain, returning to the United States only during the Spanish Civil War, and died on December 24, 1941, at the British American Hospital in Madrid. Upon her death the Byne-Stapley estate was valued at approximately $127,000 (around $2.5 million in 2024).[77] Part of the estate was auctioned on June 4 and 5, 1942, at Parke-Bernet Galleries in New York, and their house in Madrid is now the residence of the deputy chief of mission of the US embassy in Spain.[78]

Byne and Stapley left behind a complex legacy. Perceptions of their careers and roles in the sale and exportation of art from Spain have shifted over the course of the twentieth century as international standards and ethics surrounding cultural patrimony have evolved. During their lifetimes they were widely recognized as leading experts on Spanish visual culture, with dozens of publications to their names. In Spain and abroad, they were praised for increasing knowledge and appreciation of Spanish art and culture, which, in turn, promoted tourism to Spain. In 1927 they were decorated under the dictatorship of Primo de Rivera with two honors: the Civil Order of Alfonso XII for Mildred Stapley and a first-class Gran Cruz del Merito Militar (grand cross of military merit) for Arthur Byne.[79] The Mallorcan elite also celebrated Byne and Stapley for making the island's artistic treasures better known. On January 15, 1929, a banquet was held in their honor at the Hotel Victoria in Palma, where they were described as "indigenous as much as foreigners."[80] Mallorcan newspapers were among those that lamented Byne's death in 1935, as did the board of trustees of the Hispanic Society, which passed a resolution expressing "high appreciation of his most valued services to the Society and of his most distinguished career."[81]

In recent decades scholars have condemned the duo as looters who promoted a false image of themselves as dedicated Hispanists and concealed their unsavory mercantile activities from the public eye.[82] Indeed, the increase in the exportation of art from Spain that resulted from Byne and Stapley's publications was not lost on one Spanish reviewer of *Majorcan Houses and Gardens* in 1928, who wrote equivocally: "We can never thank them enough for their work of propagandizing and popularizing, above all, even though it has inevitably brought with it the painful emigration of no small number of our works of ancient art to the museums and collections of North America. The Bynes have also contributed in no small measure to the development of the studies of Spanish art in their country of origin."[83]

Upon his death Byne was described in *The New York Times* as "one of the wealthiest and most prominent" Americans in Spain.[84] The wealth he and Stapley amassed was at least in part the result of their profiting from Spain's political and economic instability. At the same time, as was the case with the Mallorcan patio elements, often the works that came to Byne's attention had already been offered unsuccessfully by Spanish dealers like Costa to potential local buyers.[85] It is also difficult to know what fate would have awaited many of the objects Byne sold had they not been purchased by American individuals and institutions, given the continued political instability in Spain in the 1930s. While there are now international legal guidelines against exporting works during periods of upheaval, a common refrain in the American press was that dealers like Byne and collectors like Hearst saved Spain's patrimony from destruction or neglect, and that is certainly an argument Byne and Stapley made in defense of their activities.[86] Responding to one Spanish critic in 1924, Stapley wrote: "He knows well the vast sum of American money spent in reclaiming for Spain historic monuments which the natives themselves have shamefully maltreated. Likewise he knows that if Spanish art is sold out of the country it is Spaniards themselves who implore foreigners to buy it, charging, always, a fantastic price for their wares."[87] In the case of the Mallorcan stairway and gallery, Stapley's final argument appears to be at least partially true: Byne could not have assembled, sold, or exported the complex without Costa, and both dealers profited handsomely from its sale to Hearst.

The Fate of Hearst's Collection

Shortly after his purchase of the Mallorcan patio elements, in the wake of the stock market crash of October 1929, Hearst began cutting back on both acquisitions and construction at San Simeon.[88] Neither the stairway and gallery nor the ceilings appear to have been sent to California; all likely remained in storage at Hearst's Bronx warehouse.[89] While Hearst may initially have intended for this patio complex to be installed in a new Los Angeles home, the last reference to the ensemble in Morgan and Byne's correspondence suggests a change in plans that would separate the stairway and gallery. In April 1930 she wrote to Byne of two new small houses in the "Recreation Wing" at San Simeon, noting that "one of the new houses embodies the Palma Majorca loggias and ceilings."[90] There is no evidence to suggest that this plan was realized, however, or that either the gallery or ceilings were ever installed at San Simeon. In May 1931 the ceilings appear in an inventory of ceilings *not* in California, with a handwritten note that they were intended for "House (E)," a guesthouse that was never constructed.[91]

Hearst's finances became increasingly tenuous around 1936, as various debts came due and boycotts of his corporation surged, fueled in part by his opposition to Franklin D. Roosevelt's New Deal and his belief that Joseph Stalin and communism posed a greater threat than Adolf Hitler, who initially received relatively friendly coverage in the Hearst papers.[92] In 1938 Hearst appointed the lawyer Clarence Shearn to reorganize his business holdings. As trustee, Shearn compelled Hearst to transfer about half his art collection to the International Studio Art Corporation, which would sell it to raise funds.[93] In order not to flood the market, sales of the collection proceeded in stages. The first sales were arranged privately with individuals and museums; these were followed by two years of private sales brokered through dealers and moderately scaled public auctions. Finally, as World War II intensified, the remainder of the collection held by the International Studio Art Corporation was auctioned in two massive New York sales held throughout 1941 and into 1942, a strategy Hearst opposed as devaluing the collection and diminishing potential proceeds.[94] With everything "priced to sell"—beginning at a mere $0.35 for an Egyptian statuette—the works on offer ranged from paintings to "whole buildings and parts of buildings ... including seventy paneled rooms taken from English, Dutch and French castles." The roughly fifteen thousand objects were put on display over 100,000 square feet at two department stores—Saks Fifth Avenue and Gimbel Brothers—and were "offered to the public like any other article or merchandise sold in department stores, with a price tag and description attached to each item."[95] The media frenzy surrounding the sales at times mocked the "liquidation prices," but newspapers also compared the collection "in quantity to the exhibition of collections as large as those of the British Museum and the Paris Louvre combined."[96] In 1951 *The New York Times* reported that Hearst's collection had been appraised between $15 million and $50 million ($320 million to $1.067 billion in 2024). In the first week

(February 1941), more than one hundred thousand people attended the sale, resulting in $500,000 ($11.2 million in 2024) in purchases.[97]

One of the items for sale that attracted significant press coverage in Spain was the Sacramenia cloister (see fig. 21). Following the announcement that it would be auctioned off, the Falange party in Spain—the sole legal political party under Franco—issued a harsh critique of Hearst and the government of the Second Republic, which had allowed the monastery to be exported. *The New York Times* reported:

> [The newspaper] Arriba, organ of the Falange, the Spanish totalitarian party, condemned Mr. Hearst as "a conceited fellow," but it voiced sharper anger at the previous regime in Spain for letting such an artistic treasure out of the country.
>
> It declared the government that allowed the sale was so immorally lacking in its duties that "we might well have lost forever Toledo, Santiago, the River Tagus and the Escorial."
>
> Hereafter, Arriba asserted, Spain would never sell "the smallest part of her old and beautiful inheritance."[98]

Less attention was given to the Mallorcan stairway and gallery, which was quietly listed in the Gimbel Brothers sale catalog under the section "Buildings and Parts: Staircases—Various Countries."[99]

European Nobility in New Jersey: The Baron and Baroness Cassel van Doorn

Hearst's 1941 sale was well timed for the recent arrival in the United States of Baron Jean Germain Léon (1882–1952) and Baroness Marij Vincentia (1911–2006) Cassel van Doorn, art collectors who had emigrated from Europe with aspirations to rebuild their collections on a grand scale. After the German invasion of France in May 1940, the couple left their estates and collections in the South of France and traveled to Lisbon, where they boarded the SS *Excambion* on November 19, 1940. They arrived in Hoboken, New Jersey, on November 29, 1940, with their two young daughters, Christiane and Jacqueline; their Algerian nurse, Mama Ziani Hogana; and their private secretary, Marguerite Pick.[100]

Jean Germain Léon Cassel belonged to a prominent Belgian family of Jewish heritage {28}.[101] His father, Léon Cassel (1853–1930), had been the head of Banque Cassel, a private bank. Formed in the early nineteenth century, Banque Cassel under Léon's leadership came to play a major role in financing Belgium's industrial development and

{28}
Baron Jean Germain Léon Cassel van Doorn, undated photograph. Cassel van Doorn Archive

{29}
Baroness Marij Vincentia Cassel van Doorn, undated photograph. Cassel van Doorn Archive

colonial expansion; in recognition of this, King Albert I bestowed upon him the title of baron in September 1929. When Léon died a few months later, his only son, Jean, inherited the title and leadership of the bank.[102] Léon was a prominent collector—in 1928 he gave a painting of Venus and Cupid by Lucas Cranach to the Royal Museums of Fine Arts of Belgium—and Jean shared his father's interest in art.[103] Marij Vincentia van Doorn was a Dutch aristocrat {29}. The couple wed in 1934 in a small civil ceremony in London. He was fifty-two and a widower; she was twenty-three.[104] They combined their last names, as was customary in Belgium.[105]

Before the war, the Cassel van Doorns had lived primarily on a property in Cannes called Le Domaine des Hespérides and were renovating the nearby Château de l'Hermitage in Cap d'Ail, which they intended to use as their winter residence.[106] The baron described their collections as wide-ranging, consisting of "pictures, drawings, prints, furniture, tapistries, rugs, carpets, china, terracottas, bronzes, glass wear, persian Rhages Sultanabab pottery, frescoes, Art reference books etc ... very valuable antique French silver and unnumerable objets of Art."[107] In 1939, "fearing trouble with the Italians on the nearby frontier," they decided to pack up much of their collection and distribute it across five major locations in southern France, using a mover named Joseph Darnard.[108] They also had considerable assets transferred to US bank accounts.[109] With the move of their collection complete and loyal colleagues, family members, and servants watching over the various storage sites, the Cassel van Doorns left for Portugal and the United States in 1940.

When they arrived in New Jersey, the couple found several short-term accommodations. They stayed at the residence of the former ambassador to France, Walter E. Edge, in Atlantic City and later in an Englewood home owned by the widow of the industrialist William Davis Ticknor.[110] During this time they seemed to be planning their next steps. On May 15, 1941, the Cassel van Doorns filed incorporation papers for "Regency, Inc.," with the stated purpose "to engage in the antique business."[111] On December 26, 1941, they purchased a property at 240 Broad Avenue in Englewood for $50,000 ($1.1 million in 2024), using funds they had deposited into the corporation's account. They named the estate Jevington Manor, perhaps a nod to one of the baron's property holdings abroad: Filching Manor, near the village of Jevington (East Sussex, England), which he purchased in 1914 and maintained from afar until his death.[112]

The Cassel van Doorns spent two years and a significant amount of money renovating their Englewood property and finally moved into the manor in February 1944. That it attracted local attention is evident from a newspaper article dispelling rumors that the queen of the Netherlands herself would live there. The baron dismissed this speculation—"The Queen is very busy at this time making plans to go back to her own Country"—but the article nevertheless noted, "Several other members of The Netherlands nobility reside in the mansion," which is described as an estate of six acres, surrounded by a nineteen-foot brick wall.[113] One can imagine that the baron made quite an impression. S. Lane Faison (Princeton MFA, 1932), an art historian and member of the Monuments, Fine Arts, and Archives (MFAA) program of the US Army, a group known as the Monuments Men, described the baron's appearance in 1946: "Tall, gray hair. Age about 60, good looking but dissipated face. Wears Legion d'Honneur ribbon. Well dressed, and obviously very wealthy."[114]

The baron and baroness were accustomed to living in grand estates, and so their desire to live in a similar residence in New Jersey is understandable. Their method of paying for the construction through Regency, Inc.—and their failure to pay contractors—led to a bankruptcy case that ultimately reached the US Supreme Court. The lawyers for the plaintiff portrayed the baron's home as a thinly veiled showroom for art dealing:

> Baron Cassel van Doorn and his wife are Europeans with a long background of wealth, culture and taste. They rescued a substantial part of their fortune from war-torn Belgium

> and came to America in 1940. The van Doorns conceived an ambitious, albeit impracticable, program for entry into the commercial wealth of this country. The Baron had always been a great lover of and authority on antiques although he had never been in the business for profit.... Taking a leaf from the book of some of the commercially successful antiquarians, he planned a pretentious showplace near New York in which various rooms would be paneled and furnished to authoritatively represent periods of European antiquity and therein display for possible customers the items he had for sale.... Such place would also be his home to which he would invite people of means to parties, dinners and as house guests and thus indirectly show off his wares even to the extent of interesting people in the purchase of whole rooms and balconies, mantle pieces and paneling imported from Europe. The actual business of buying and selling would then be conducted from an office in New York City.[115]

The Cassel van Doorns strongly opposed this characterization, insisting that the home was always and only intended to be a residence. Responding to these accusations, they went so far as to itemize in court documents their expenditures on their kitchen renovation.

While their reasons for the construction of their residence may not be certain, as work there was just beginning or perhaps even earlier, the baron was already making his presence known in the New York art world. In May 1941 he attended the sale of Sarah Jones Walters, the widow of the businessman and art collector Henry Walters, where he outbid prominent collectors including J. Paul Getty on an eighteenth-century writing table now in the Metropolitan Museum of Art.[116] Given that he purchased art at the sale of one legendary American collector shortly after arriving in the country, it is perhaps not surprising that he visited Hearst's New York sales. There it seems he purchased not only the Mallorcan stairway and gallery, accompanied by its Bronx inventory records, but also a window from the Vaucluse region of France now in Princeton's collections {30}.

The Mallorcan patio elements were installed in the gardens of Jevington Manor in the 1940s, with the stairs leading up to the balustrades and columns lining an open gallery on the second level in an arrangement that diverges from Byne's renderings, offering a

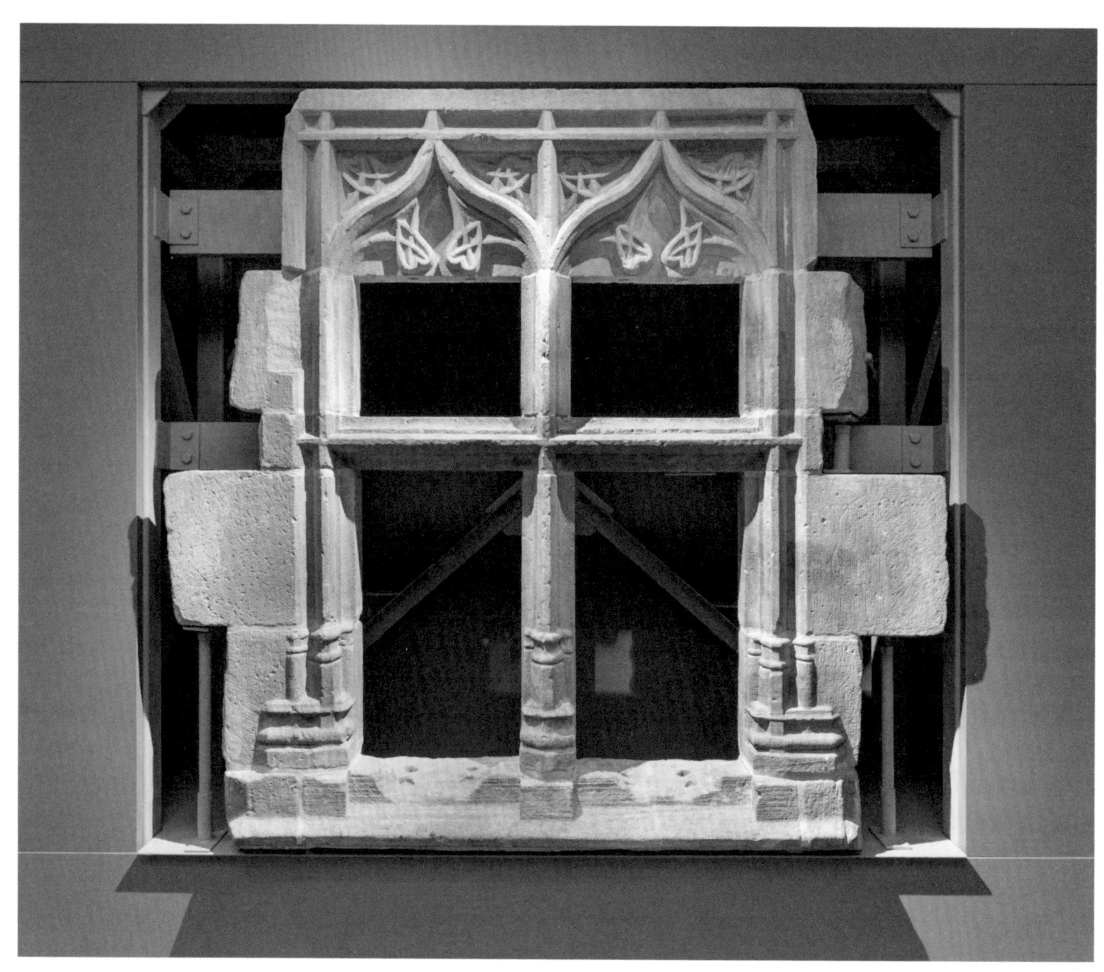

{30}
Vaucluse, France, Window, 15th century. Princeton University Art Museum. Gift of Baroness Cassel van Doorn (y1955-3286)

reinterpretation of the elements to suit their new context {31}. A few years later they were joined by a partial limestone cloister formed of medieval French and Spanish elements and designed by George Grey Barnard {32}.[117] While these purchases—and their installation—might seem to lend credence to the claim that the baron and baroness had contemplated turning their Englewood home into a showroom of "whole rooms and balconies, mantle pieces and paneling imported from Europe," it seems equally possible that they were attempting to replicate in atmosphere and substance the collections and residences they had left behind in Europe.

Indeed, the baron's collecting in these early years in New York was varied and ranged across media, time periods, and geographies, including a twelfth-century seated Guanyin from the late Northern Song dynasty as well as a sixteenth-century Flemish tapestry. The Princeton University Art Museum holds two paintings and a sculpture that the baron acquired in New York in these early years: the reclining Spanish knight in armor, or *gisant* {33}, purchased at the 1941 Parke-Bernet sale of the railroad industrialist Arthur Curtiss James; a fifteenth-century painting of Saint Francis by the Italian artist Antonio Leonelli {34}, purchased at a 1942 sale of paintings from the collection of the Mexican politician Alberto J. Pani; and Jean-Léon Gérôme's *Napoleon in Egypt* (1867–68) {35}, likely purchased at a 1943 Parke-Bernet sale from the collection of the dealer Frank G. Schnittjer.

The baron's vigorous activities on the New York market attracted the attention not only of collectors, dealers, and auction houses but also of the Federal Bureau of Investigation (FBI). In a 1946 letter FBI Director J. Edgar Hoover wrote: "Francis H. Taylor, Director of the Metropolitan Museum of Art, New York City, mentioned in an interview that one Baron De Cassel of Englewood, New Jersey, purports to be a Belgian refugee. According to Mr. Taylor, De Cassel was brought to his attention when he attempted at one time to corner the auction trade in New York City. He stated De Cassel's dealings are very suspicious and that his activities are known to members of the Parr Bennett [Parke Bernet] Galleries in New York City."[118] Although it is difficult to know what Taylor meant by "suspicious" activities, it is certainly true that the baron was acquiring prodigiously and visibly from auction houses and New York dealers in the early 1940s. Nonetheless, the prominent place given to the Mallorcan stairway and gallery at Jevington Manor suggests its importance in building a new identity for the Cassel van Doorns as European nobility living in the United States.

{31}
Mallorcan stairway and gallery, installed at Jevington Manor, Englewood, New Jersey, ca. 1944–55. Cassel van Doorn Archive

{32}
George Grey Barnard (1863–1938; born Bellefonte, PA; died New York, NY), partial limestone cloister, installed at Jevington Manor, ca. 1944–55. Cassel van Doorn Archive

{33}
Artist unidentified, Spain, *Gisant: Knight in Armor*, ca. 1500. Alabaster, 63.5 × 189.9 × 43.3 cm. Princeton University Art Museum. Gift of Baroness Cassel van Doorn (y1955-3277)

{34}
Antonio Leonelli (active 1478–before 1525, Italy), *Saint Francis*, 1490s. Tempera on wood panel, 74.5 × 56 cm. Princeton University Art Museum. Museum purchase, Carl Otto von Kienbusch Jr. Memorial Collection (y1956-3)

{35}
Jean-Léon Gérôme (1824–1904; born Vesoul, France; died Paris, France), *Napoleon in Egypt*, 1867–68. Oil on wood panel, 35.8 × 25 cm. Princeton University Art Museum. Museum purchase, John Maclean Magie, Class of 1892, and Gertrude Magie Fund (y1953-78)

Aktion Berta

Even as he was amassing a new collection in New Jersey, the baron was also working for the restitution of his family's collection formed in Europe, which had been systematically looted during the war. His efforts transformed Jevington Manor into an estate housing both old and new collections, assembled in Europe and the United States before, during, and after World War II.

The Nazis had long identified the Cassel van Doorn collection as a target, and on March 18, 1942, an administrator from the Commissariat of Jewish Assets and two police officers arrived at the Domaine des Hespérides to seize it. Jean Louis de Ricqlès, secretary-general of Banque Cassel, was staying at the estate and was able to dissuade them, insisting on launching a formal appeal to prove the baron's "Aryan" status under Nazi racial laws—a process that dragged on until May 1943. Nonetheless, in December 1943 the SD (*Sicherheitsdiesnt*), the Nazi intelligence agency, and the collaborationist Vichy police seized the Cassel van Doorn collection, which had been scattered across southern France. Ricqlès recounted:

> The man in charge said that M. Cassel was 100% Jewish. I wanted to show a copy of the parentage papers proving that under French law, M. Cassel could not be considered as Jewish, as well as a copy of the order relieving the commissioner of his duties. I was told that these papers did not interest them, that

M. Cassel had been naturalized as an American Jew, that he was in dissent and that they had seen, regarding this naturalization, a note on the desk of M. Darquier de Pellequoi [likely Louis Darquier de Pellepoix, commissioner for Jewish affairs]. On arriving, they already knew my name, knew that I had M. Cassel's belongings at my house.... He pretended to carry a warrant for my arrest but did not show it to me.... I was only able to save a box where I had gathered what seemed to me the best in terms of drawings and engravings, between their two visits and which I had hidden in a clothing closet. As they left, they asked for the certificates of parentage that I had wanted to show them and took them away. Trucks (ten to twelve) ... came to make the move. They were accompanied by around thirty Germans.[119]

It became apparent that the Nazis knew the collection in intimate detail because the mover whom the baron had used in 1939, Darnard, had become a far-right extremist and the de facto leader of the Milice Française, a pro-Nazi paramilitary organization under the Vichy regime. Darnard later swore an oath of loyalty to Hitler and became an officer in the ss (*Schutzstaffel*), the Nazi paramilitary organization. After the war, he was tried for collaboration with the enemy and executed.[120] The baron—who had received accounts of the looting from friends, family members, and employees—explained:

When we sent our furniture from Cannes to the Ardèche, in 1939, the removal firm of Joseph Darnard, 56, rue Gioffredo, Nice, was recommanded [*sic*] to us with the result that this now famous or rather infamous man, who has since been shot by the French, knew exactly where our collections had been shipped and had a complete list of them.... In view of this person's activities during the war, it is most probable that all this information was also conveyed to the Germans, for they appeared to know exactly the location of everything we possessed in the South of France, in Vals and in Ruoms.[121]

The Nazis assigned the code name Aktion Berta to the Cassel van Doorn collection and sent it to the Altaussee salt mines and Schloss Thürnthal in Austria—key storage sites for looted art destined for Hitler's unrealized Führermuseum in Linz, an ambitious project meant to celebrate "Aryan" art. A report on the transport authored by

Monuments Man Faison reveals the vast extent of the looting:

> *The "Aktion* BERTA*"* (Baron CASSEL Collection): In March 1944, a transport of 18 railway cars, loaded with boxes and crates marked with the code name "BERTA," arrived at Bad Aussee. The train had come from France.... As the contents were largely household goods of small value, even including kitchen utensils, it was decided to store only the more valuable portions at Alt Aussee (where space was at a premium), and to ship the remainder to Schloss Thürnthal, Niederdonau. The most valuable part was a group of French paintings of the late 19th Century. The whole collection was appraised by Oskar HAMEL of Vienna at some 1,500,000 reichsmarks [approximately $10.85 million in 2024].[122]

A 1945 German inventory of the Altaussee salt mines indicates that 409 paintings and 240 works on paper, furniture, tapestries, and other objects from the Cassel van Doorn collection were stored there {36}.[123]

After the war, many of the baron's looted possessions were sent to the Musée du Jeu de Paume in Paris, which was the processing center for objects from MFAA collecting points in Germany. In 1946 the baron began working with the MFAA and French officials on the restitution of his collection to the United States.[124] In the end, of the 3,478 works of art from the Cassel van Doorn collection, 988 were repatriated to France and one to Belgium.[125] Restitutions have continued since then;

{36}
Two men standing by racks of paintings inside a salt mine in Altaussee, Austria, ca. 1945. Archives of American Art, Smithsonian Institution, Washington, DC. Andrew Carnduff Ritchie papers, 1907–1983

EDMONTON, ALBERTA, TUESDAY, DECEMBER 5, 1950

MISSING TREASURE PACKED

QUILTED CLOCK receives the treatment worthy of a Belgian art treasure. One of 32 objects of art worth $40,000 stolen from Belgian nobleman's estate during the war, it is being specially packed by C. L. Cudmore in Big Four Storage warehouse for shipment to Englewood, N.J., home of Baron Cassel van Doorn. Art treasures were brought to Edmonton in August, 1949, and recovered here 13 months later.

{37}
"Missing Treasure Packed," *Edmonton Bulletin*, December 5, 1950

in 2014, for example, the French government restituted to the heirs of the Cassel van Doorns a painting by the seventeenth-century Flemish artist Joos de Momper, *Mountain Landscape (with Chapel)*, which had been stored in the Altaussee mine.[126]

The Cassel van Doorns also had a collection in Belgium whose fate during World War II came to light not through governmental restitution processes but instead through an improbable transatlantic insurance fraud scheme. According to Canadian news reports, in August 1949 a Belgian citizen named Lucien Bral arrived in St. Albert, a small city in Alberta, seeking a fire insurance policy for an art collection valued at $73,560 ($966,000 in 2024). That very night a fire broke out in the temporary storage quarters housing the collection. The fire was quickly extinguished, with minimal damage to the collection, but Bral's subsequent insurance claim spurred a search for the true owner of the collection, which some months later was determined to be Baron Cassel van Doorn. One news source recounted that a trusted servant, Jules Tutelaire, had removed much of the art from the baron's home in Belgium when it was occupied by the Nazis and seemed to have made a deal with Bral.[127] In 1950 the collection—which included paintings by John Singer Sargent, Henri Fantin-Latour, Jules Breton, and others—was returned to the Cassel van Doorns in New Jersey, joining the Mallorcan stairway and gallery and the many other works of art and architecture they had assembled {37}.

The Cassel van Doorn Gift to Princeton

The baron died on July 19, 1952; at his death his collection in New Jersey was valued at $703,700 ($8.4 million in 2024).[128] Shortly thereafter, the baroness began liquidating much of the collection they had amassed, selling at auctions in New York and Paris.[129] In the mid-1950s she also began making donations to museums in the United States and Europe. Her donations to American museums appear to have been primarily architectural elements, such as the Mallorcan stairway and gallery.

It is only with the baron's death that the baroness emerges in the historical record with greater clarity. Ernest DeWald (Class of 1914, 1916), who served as director of the Art Museum from 1946 to 1960, described her fondly: "She is an extremely charming and cultured Continental lady who at one time considered living here at Princeton."[130] The collector and Princeton alumnus and benefactor Carl Otto Kretzschmar von Kienbusch (Class of 1906) facilitated the donation of several objects from the Cassel van Doorn collection to Princeton, including the Mallorcan patio elements. In 1963 he recounted the story of the gift to Patrick J. Kelleher (Graduate School Class of 1942, 1947), who served as the Museum's director from 1960 to 1972:

> I had known the Baroness van Doorn as a lovely lady for a number of years.... The Baron Van Doorn was a Dutch-Belgian emigre who came to the United States because of some jewish [*sic*] blood which the Hitler element didn't like. He brought a lot of money with him, settled in Englewood where he built a very expensive house surrounded by a garden which was surrounded by a brick wall. He began buying antiques of the Medieval, Gothic and Renaissance periods from such dealers as Joe Brummer. Principly [*sic*] he was interested in architectural stones. These he set up in his Englewood home or in the garden surrounding it.... When her husband died she gave a considerable amount of material from the garden and from storage to the Cloisters at the request of Jimmy Rorimer [director of the Metropolitan Museum, 1955–66]. She asked me what I would like to have for myself, thinking I would want the tomb figure of the armored knight [the *gisant*; see fig. 33].... I told the Baroness that, much as I appreciated her kind intentions toward me, I had no place to put this figure except in

the garden back of my house where it would suffer from the climate. I suggested that she give it to Princeton. She agreed and Ernest DeWald paid her a visit at my suggestion. Ernest and the Baroness got along very nicely, with the result that between Ernest and myself we managed to get a great deal more than just the armored figure. In fact, we got so much that Harold Dodds [president of Princeton University, 1933–57] spent a lot of time worrying where to store it. Put together it should make a magnificent room and balcony in the Gothic tradition.[131]

The baroness's suggestion that Kienbusch might want the *gisant* suggests a relatively close relationship between the two: Kienbusch had assembled perhaps the finest private collection of European arms and armor, which he donated to the Philadelphia Museum of Art upon his death, and this sculpture of a reclining knight in armor certainly would have found appropriate context in his collection. Carved of porous and delicate alabaster, however, it would not have fared well in Kienbusch's garden; happily, it instead joined the baroness's gifts to Princeton, along with the Mallorcan stairway and gallery, the window from the Vaucluse mentioned previously, as well as three French doorways, two wood sculptures, and a stone window from Rozérieulles (Moselle).[132] Kienbusch's statement that combining these elements would "make a magnificent room and balcony in the Gothic tradition" indicates that, once again, the stairway and gallery were valued more as being representative of an aesthetic and architectural type rather than as an ensemble with its own history.

Dodds's concerns about storage were not unfounded. Kienbusch covered the cost of transporting the architectural elements donated by the baroness to Princeton, where the Mallorcan stairway and gallery were stored in the "Crystal Room" under Nassau Hall from September 1955 until July 1963.[133] The Mallorcan patio elements and many of the baroness's other gifts were ultimately incorporated, as Kienbusch had suggested, into the medieval gallery of the Museum building that opened in 1966 {38}. It seems that some parts of the structure may have been lost along the way: Although both the ensemble's accession card and Byne's drawings mention two windows, these were not installed in the new Museum, and their current whereabouts remain unknown. Similarly, the two ceilings that Hearst purchased from Byne were sold at his auction in New York but have not reappeared since.

The baroness never saw the stairway and gallery installed at Princeton. Following the execution of the baron's will in 1956, she

{38}
Mallorcan gallery, installed in the Princeton University Art Museum, after 1966

inherited half of the estate, totaling $1,213,000 ($14.2 million in 2024). The remaining half was divided between their three daughters (14% each) and Marguerite Pick (8%), the Cassel van Doorns' secretary, who had traveled with them to the United States in 1940. In the mid-1950s the baroness and her family moved to Chile, following her eldest daughter's marriage to a Chilean. By the late 1950s the baroness had moved to Germany, where she remarried. Marguerite Pick remained in New York and managed the estate's affairs, including the dispersal of the gifts to Princeton. In 1958 the Orthodox Congregation Ahavath Torah purchased the forty-three-room Jevington Manor for $55,000 ($606,000 in 2024) and turned it into a synagogue and Hebrew school, which remains there to this day.[134]

Hoping to invite the baroness to the opening of the new Museum building, in 1965 Patick Kelleher was in touch with Marguerite Pick, who had since become an interior designer in New York City. She could not provide an address for the baroness but offered to forward a message from Kelleher. He in turn provided a letter earnestly describing the value of the baroness's gifts to Princeton: "The stone-work adds such distinction to the medieval and renaissance galleries that it would give us a great deal of pleasure to show you how beautifully your generous gift is being employed for the eventual pleasure and enjoyment of generations to come."[135]

Displayed in the Entrance Hall of the new Princeton University Art Museum in an arrangement that echoes their installation at Jevington Manor, the stairway and gallery once again can be studied by generations of Museum visitors. Now recognized as forming a composite object assembled in the 1920s, the individual elements can be appreciated as a testament to the beauty and accomplishment of fifteenth- and sixteenth-century Mallorcan architectural sculpture. Together, the stairway and gallery serve as an impressive reminder of how the early twentieth-century American fascination for Spain fueled the creation of large-scale hybrid ensembles in which Spanish architecture was reimagined and transported to the United States.

Stairway probably from
Carrer de l'Aigua (Water Street)
15th–16th century

Gallery (balustrades and columns)
from Can Ayamans (Ayamans House)
16th century

Palma de Mallorca, Spain
Limestone
Gift of Baroness Cassel van Doorn
y1955-3282 a–b

These architectural elements come from at least two grand residences in the Mediterranean island city of Palma de Mallorca. Together, they offer a rare surviving example of a classic feature of fifteenth- and sixteenth-century Mallorcan architecture: the interior patio, in which an outdoor stairway leads to a second-story open-air gallery lined with balustrades and columns.

Due to shifting tastes and urbanization projects, these architectural fragments were removed from their original settings in the late nineteenth and early twentieth centuries. In the 1920s, during a time of American fascination with Spain, they were combined by two art dealers in Palma—Josep Costa Ferrer and Arthur Byne—and sold as a single Mallorcan patio to the newspaper magnate William Randolph Hearst, who intended to use them to adorn a home he planned to build in Los Angeles.

The elements were shipped to Hearst's warehouse in the Bronx in 1929, but they never continued westward. Instead, he sold them in 1941, and they entered the collection of Baron and Baroness Cassel van Doorn, who had fled Europe during World War II. The Cassel van Doorns integrated the gallery and stairway into their home in Englewood, New Jersey. In 1955, following the baron's death, the baroness donated them to the Princeton University Art Museum.

E CANTA SON MAL
DONCEL QVE BALL

ME IOS HOMENS

ELENA TOROK

The Installation History of Princeton's Mallorcan Stairway and Gallery, ca. 1925–2025

For more than half a century, little was known about the stairway and gallery from Mallorca installed in the Princeton University Art Museum's gallery of medieval art. In 2020 the Museum began to formulate plans to dismantle and move the architectural grouping in advance of its new building project. After deinstallation in 2021 a conservation treatment to prepare the work for transition to a new space also sparked collaborative research and physical examination that shed new light on its provenance, design, and historical context.

During the Museum's five-year closure from 2020 to 2025, novel discoveries regarding the grouping's past became critical in shaping decisions for its future. The twentieth-century journey of these elements from Mallorca to Princeton, as outlined earlier in this volume, included four transfers of ownership and installations in three different locations. When architectural works are moved, changes to their appearance, configuration, and condition can influence how we interpret their history.

In preparing for the assemblage's current display (see pp. 76–77), the Museum was presented with several complex questions: Which (if any) of the previous configurations most accurately reflected the historical origins of the stairway and gallery? If this could not be determined or if it was not possible to restore it to the way it looked during a specific era, how should the elements be displayed in the future? And finally, what factors would need to be accounted for in these decisions?

Answering these questions required close partnership with EverGreene Architectural Arts, which collaborated on the deinstallation of the stairway and gallery and their installation in the new Museum building while also overseeing the conservation project carried out in the interim. During the conservation treatment the Museum's curators and conservators worked with the specialists at EverGreene to reassess the elements' material history, installation records, and past restorations. This essay examines the stairway and gallery's previous installations in detail, with a focus on how the overall configuration and the individual elements have changed over time, as well as how this new understanding guided decisions for current display.

History and Composition

Today the stairway and gallery consist of more than one hundred individual carved limestone elements (see fig. 7), including eight stairway panels and associated railings, four full and two half (formerly engaged) columns with bases and capitals, eighteen balusters, five newel posts, and three newel-post toppers (including two flat and one with a grotesque).[1] With the exception of four newel posts and the flat toppers, all elements originate from at least two different houses in historic Palma de Mallorca. The gallery elements are from Can Ayamans on Carrer d'en Morei, and the stairway elements are likely from a house that once stood on Carrer de l'Aigua.[2] The carved decorations on elements from each location are markedly different in style: Columns from Can Ayamans contain features consistent with the sixteenth century, including ornamental motifs such as garlands of fruit, draped fabric, and portraits, alongside more symbolic or allegorical elements such as masks, animal skulls, and archery equipment (bows and quivers) {39}. In contrast, the stairway panels from Carrer de l'Aigua feature elements more typical of the late fifteenth and early sixteenth centuries, including circular Gothic tracery and inscribed banderoles (scroll-like forms bearing carved text, which may have served both decorative and devotional functions) (see pp. 78–79).

As Alexandra Letvin details in her essay in this volume, even though the individual elements are centuries old, the group as it exists today was formed only in the 1920s, through the efforts of the Spanish artist and dealer Josep Costa Ferrer (Picarol) (1876–1971) and the American architect, artist, and art dealer Arthur Byne (1884–1935).[3]

{39}
Carved details on Mallorcan gallery columns originating from Can Ayamans

The gallery components from Can Ayamans, likely removed from their original context sometime in the late nineteenth century, were acquired in Mallorca in 1925 by Costa, who worked in the following years to oversee a major restoration to prepare the elements for sale. In 1929, after Costa was unable to find a local buyer, he sold the gallery elements to Byne.[4] At some point later that year, and with involvement from both men, a stairway (likely from Carrer de l'Aigua) was added to the gallery elements from Can Ayamans to form a singular composition that could adorn a two-story open courtyard or patio, a traditional feature of many *casas señoriales* in Mallorca and Spain. Byne sold the composition to the American collector and publishing magnate William Randolph Hearst (1863–1951).[5] Hearst never installed the stairway or gallery at any of his properties, and they were eventually sold during the liquidation of the International Studio Art Corporation (a subsidiary of Hearst Corporation) in 1941.[6] By 1942 the elements were in the possession of Baron Jean Germain Léon Cassel van Doorn (1882–1952) and Baroness Marij Vincentia Cassel van Doorn (1911–2006), who installed them outdoors at their estate in Englewood, New Jersey, where they remained until 1955, when the baroness donated them to Princeton University.[7] The stairway and gallery were installed in the Princeton University Art Museum's former building from 1965 to 2021 and then in the Museum's new building in late 2024.

Examination of the elements during the recent conservation treatment revealed stone repairs that could have been applied while the stairway and gallery were still in their original locations, such as dutchman repairs, a technique used to patch smaller damages using a custom-cut insert {40}. Extensive application of twentieth-century materials was also noted, including fills, paints, washes, mortars, plasters, cements, resins, and machine-made pins {41}. Furthermore, alterations had been made to align pieces that did not appear to originally connect. Profiles and surfaces of multiple stones had been paired-in, a technique used to marry and align adjacent profiles and planes that involved the trimming and cutting of elements, followed by application of secondary fill materials to create seamless lines.[8] Identifying the exact timing of these interventions proved difficult, as many stone installation and repair techniques have remained relatively consistent since the early twentieth century. By cross-referencing material evidence with archival records, however, it was possible to construct a clearer timeline of modifications. Recognizing these differences was fundamental to both conservation work and

{40}
Three dutchman repairs (indicated by yellow arrows) to a Mallorcan gallery balustrade railing originating from Can Ayamans

{41}
Examples of materials applied during past campaigns of restoration and installation, including mortar and pins (above) and paints and washes (below)

installation planning, as it allowed the Museum to disentangle the composite nature of the ensemble and reframe it as a complex, layered artifact rather than a unified original.

Forming an Architectural Composition, 1925–29

Between 1925 and 1929 Costa oversaw restoration of both the gallery elements (from Can Ayamans) and the stairway elements (likely from Carrer de l'Aigua) to prepare them for their eventual sale. The restoration work was performed by the Mallorcan sculptor Miguel Sacanell, who worked on other city projects involving architectural preservation.[9]

Details of Sacanell's work are scarcely documented. His involvement in the restoration of the gallery elements is noted only briefly in Costa's recollections of the project published by Luis Ripoll in 1963, and there is mention of the artist's work on the stairway elements in a 1929 letter from Byne to Costa.[10] On the following pages, a comparison of historical photographs and drawings of the individual patio elements in their original contexts prior to Sacanell's restoration to four drawings Byne prepared for Hearst in 1929 {42} {43} {44} {45}, makes it clear that the modifications were extensive.

Can Ayamans once contained at least two patios that were decorated with sixteenth-century stonework, the first located at the main entryway to the residence on Carrer d'en Morei and the second located directly behind it {46}.[11] Each patio included a second-level gallery—a covered passage with an open side facing the courtyard—that was lined with columns and balustrades. As detailed earlier in this volume, this sixteenth-century stonework was commissioned by Felip Fuster after 1531 and might have been carved by Joan de Salas or his workshop.

At least two nineteenth-century photographs of the first patio survive: One is from 1895 {47},[12] and the other is not dated but appears to have also been taken around the same time {48}.[13] Both photographs show the eastern side of the space. For the second, inner patio, multiple images from the nineteenth century also exist: Four engravings were published by Archduke Ludwig Salvator of Austria in his seminal volumes on the Balearic Islands {49} {50}, a photoengraving by Joarizti and Mariezcurrena was published by Pablo Piferrer and José María Quadrado in 1888 (see fig. 1), and a drawing by Antonio Ribas Oliver was published by Álvaro Campaner y Fuertes in 1881 {51}.[14]

Can Ayamans stands today in renovated condition. Although most of the sixteenth-century elements from the patios were dismantled in the late nineteenth century (and are now part of the composition in Princeton), vestiges remain embedded.

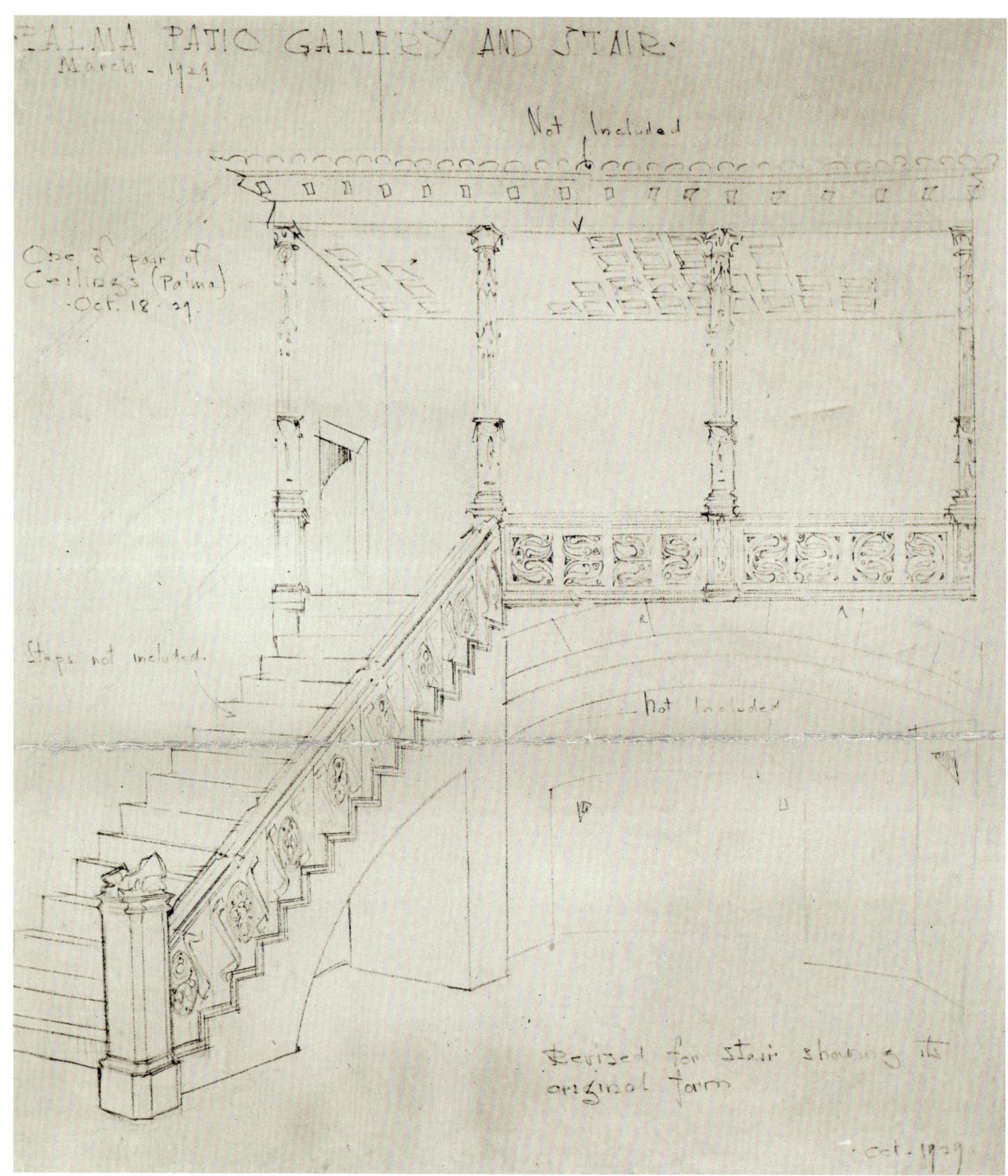
ALMA PATIO GALLERY AND STAIR.
March - 1929
Not Included
One of pair of
Ceilings (Palma)
Oct. 18 - 29.
Steps not included.
Not Included
Revised for stair showing its
original form
Oct. 1929

{42}
Arthur Byne, "Palma Patio Gallery and Stair," 1929. Photograph of a now-lost drawing in the International Studio Art Corporation's Inventory Album 83. Princeton University Art Museum, Curatorial Files

{43}
Arthur Byne, "Palma Stair," 1929. Photograph of a now-lost drawing in the International Studio Art Corporation's Inventory Album 83. Princeton University Art Museum, Curatorial Files

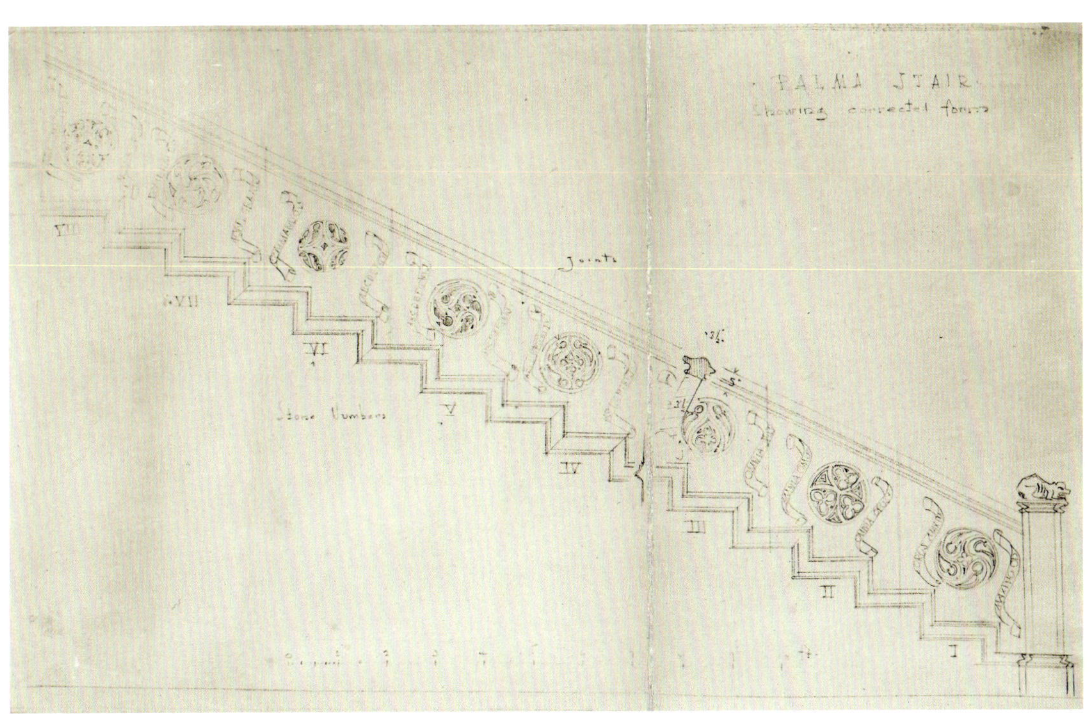

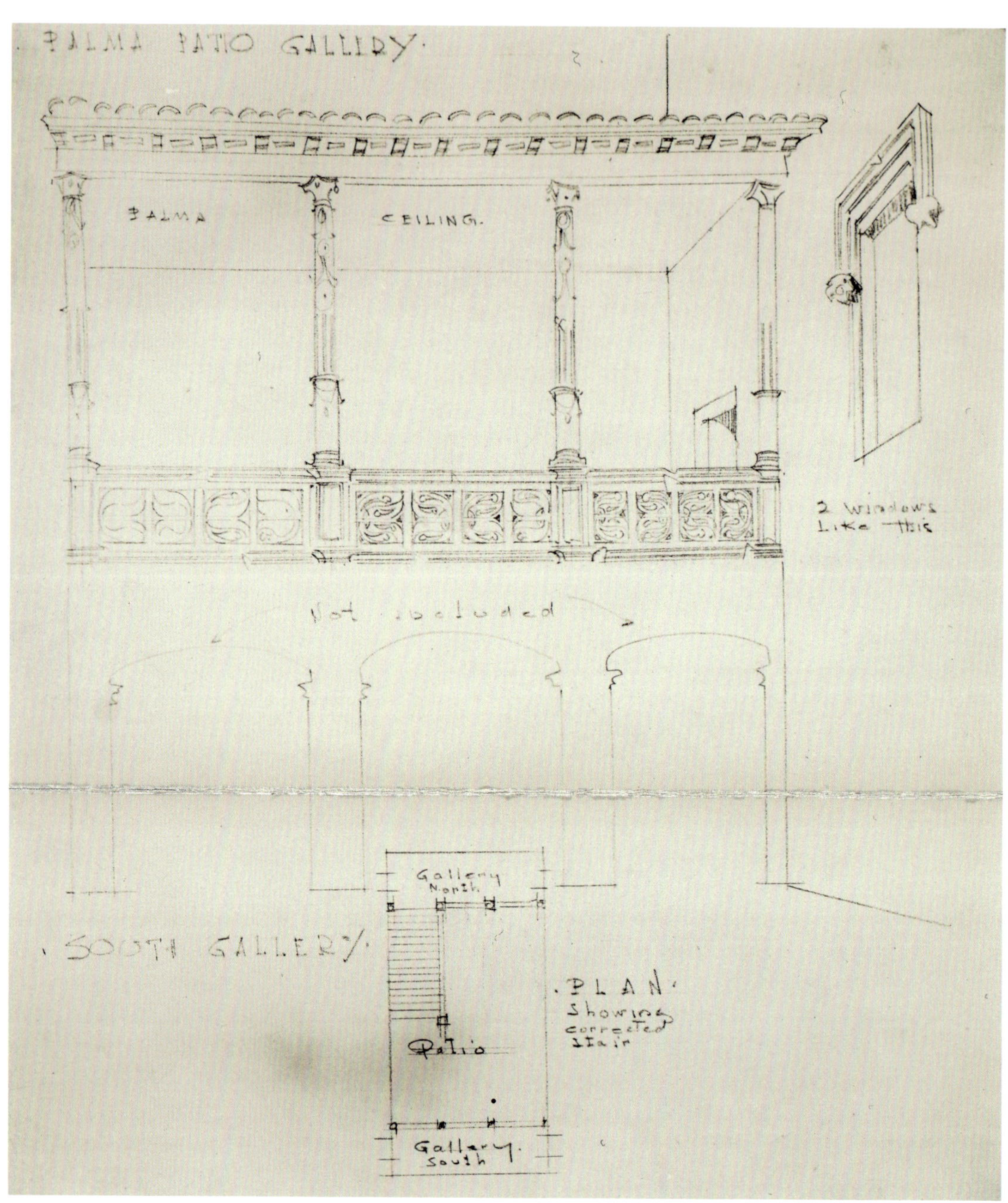
PALMA PATIO GALLERY.
PALMA
CEILING.
2 windows
Like this
Not included
SOUTH GALLERY.
Gallery
North
PLAN.
Showing
corrected
stair
Patio
Gallery.
South

{44}
Arthur Byne, "Palma Patio Gallery," 1929. Photograph of a now-lost drawing in the International Studio Art Corporation's Inventory Album 83. Princeton University Art Museum, Curatorial Files

{45}
Arthur Byne, "Palma Patio Details," 1929. Photograph of a now-lost drawing in the International Studio Art Corporation's Inventory Album 83. Princeton University Art Museum, Curatorial Files

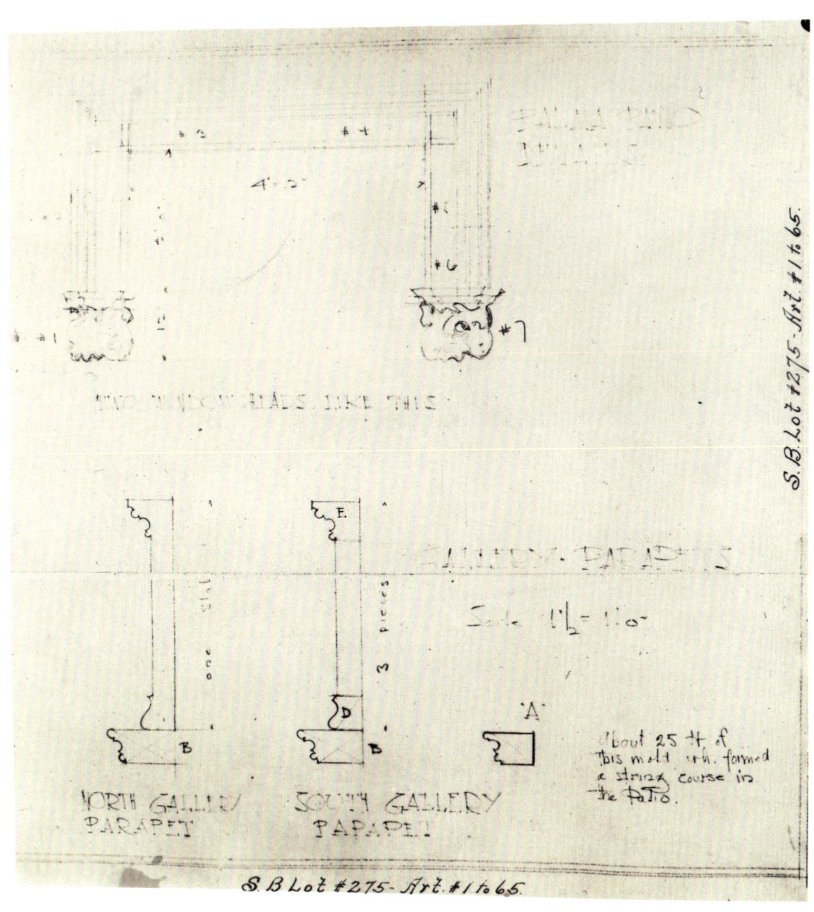

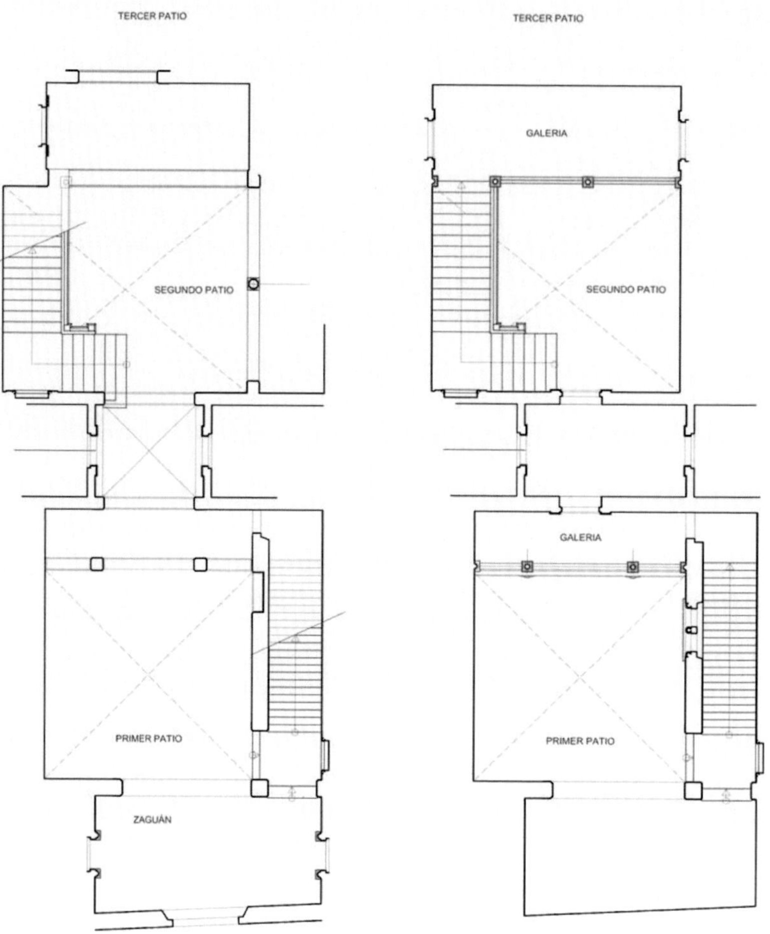

{46}
José Miguel Merino de Cáceres, reimagined floor plan of the patios of Can Ayamans, in José Miguel Merino de Cáceres and María José Martínez Ruiz, "Arthur Byne, Mildred Stapley, José Costa y el patio de la Casa Ayamans (Palma de Mallorca): Detalles de un despojo artístico en el contexto de la promoción turística balear," *Espacio, tiempo y forma* 7, no. 10 (2022)

{47}
The first patio of Can Ayamans, 1895, from a photographic album prepared by the Ciaudo family, who documented their stay in Mallorca

{48}
The first patio of Can Ayamans, n.d. This photograph was taken sometime before the gallery elements were dismantled in the late 19th century, from the family album of José María Marco

{49}
The second, inner patio of Can Ayamans. Engraving in Archduke Ludwig Salvator of Austria, *Die Balearen*, vol. 4 (Leipzig, 1882)

{50}
The second, inner patio of Can Ayamans. Engraving in Archduke Ludwig Salvator of Austria, *Die Balearen*, vol. 4 (Leipzig, 1882)

{51}
The second, inner patio of Can Ayamans. Antonio Ribas Oliver, drawing in Álvaro Campaner y Fuertes, *Cronicon Mayoricense: Noticias y relaciones históricas de Mallorca desde 1229 a 1800* (Palma de Mallorca, 1881)

{52}
Four full column bases originating from Can Ayamans; two contain a six-pointed star

{53}
Door lintel originating from Can Ayamans. Museu de Mallorca, Palma (DA05/14/0056)

The sixteenth-century elements that remain in Can Ayamans—including one door lintel, multiple door elements, at least one window, and multiple capitals—share visual similarities with those now in Princeton.[15] The door lintel is inscribed *PER UN TAL BE REPOS TINDRA ME VIDA*, interpreted as a promise of freedom made to stonemasons as a reward for their work.[16] The capitals remaining in the house have carved cartouches that were once decorated with six-pointed stars, one of the heraldic symbols of the Fuster family.[17] Though these cartouches have since been reduced to flat, blank surfaces, the same six-pointed star still adorns many of the column bases that are part of the group of elements at Princeton today {52}. One of two dismantled lintels from Can Ayamans in the collections of the Museu de Mallorca, Palma, also contains a six-pointed star {53}.[18]

In addition to heraldic symbols, three column bases now in Princeton contain cartouches with carved inscriptions. As mentioned earlier in this publication, one cartouche is inscribed with the date 1549, and this is the only inscription that remains legible (see p. 85). Whether or not this date corresponds to the completion of the patios or perhaps to another historical event is not known today. Two other column bases also once bore inscriptions that have since been removed {54}. The wear and condition of the stone in the area where the inscriptions had been suggest that this removal might have occurred before Sacanell's restoration campaign in the 1920s, perhaps while the elements were still installed in the patios of Can Ayamans.

If one compares the patio elements in the historical images of Can Ayamans (see figs. 1, 47–51) with the elements that now make up the architectural composition in Princeton, it is clear that Princeton houses a mix of columns and balustrades from the galleries of both patios. Indeed, some elements from the first patio are even joined with elements from the second. Byne rendered only a single patio for Hearst in 1929, with columns and balustrades arranged into two second-level galleries that face each other, which he labeled as a "north" gallery and a “south” gallery. His drawing of the “north” gallery resembles the layout of the eastern side of Can Ayamans’s inner patio (yet with a different staircase) (see fig. 42), and his drawing of the “south” gallery resembles the layout of the eastern side of Can Ayamans’s entryway patio (but with columns and balustrades spaced differently from the sixteenth-century arrangement) (see fig. 44). Given that Byne was working decades after the patios had been dismantled, he might have had access to the house but likely relied on historical sources more than firsthand observation.

Although the decorative carvings in the elements of each patio are very similar, there are also some notable differences. For example, there are two distinct types of molding profiles along the lower edges of the balustrade sections; one has a concave roll mold while the other does not. These differences are not visible when the elements are installed because all lower edges were filled and skim coated with restoration materials to create a uniform appearance as part of one or more twentieth-century campaigns of repair.[19] The different molding profiles can be seen from the sides of the balusters when the composition is dismantled. In fact, Byne rendered two different types of molding profiles in one of his drawings for Hearst (see fig. 45). There are also distinct carving differences between columns. The composition includes six columns overall: four full and two half (which were formerly installed against a wall in Can Ayamans). Of the full columns, two are carved in the round, while two are not. This evidence suggests that the galleries of the entryway patio and the inner patio were similar yet not identical: The balustrades differed in their lower molding profiles, and only one of the two galleries contained columns that were carved in the round.

Furthermore, the galleries in each patio had different spacing arrangements of columns and balustrades. The entryway patio had unevenly spaced columns (1 engaged column—3 balusters—1 full column—6 balusters—1 full column—3 balusters—1 engaged column), while the inner patio had evenly spaced columns (1 full column—4 balusters—1 full column—4 balusters—1 engaged column). In Byne’s 1929 drawings for Hearst, the spacing is rendered more like the latter, and the balusters were grouped and joined into balustrades by Sacanell accordingly (see figs. 42, 44).

Sacanell’s work involved the joining of multiple elements that were not adjacent to one another when installed in Can Ayamans. This is evident in the balustrades as well as in the columns. Balusters contain two different types of carved openwork, and each type was present in

{54}
Two column bases originating from Can Ayamans, showing carved cartouches with inscriptions that are no longer legible

both galleries. When elements were combined, however, some baluster elements were joined with others in ways that put different designs directly next to each other, making these differences very noticeable (see pp. 76–77). One balustrade section joins two similarly carved balusters side by side, creating a noticeably asymmetrical arrangement {55}, a configuration not visible in historical photographs but partially echoed in Byne's 1929 drawings (see fig. 42).[20] The balusters were likely grouped this way for sale because the dismantled group of elements Costa acquired in 1925 did not include a matching number of each openwork type, and since the balusters are carved on only one side, they also could not be reversed. Additionally, some column sections have also been mixed: One half column contains distinctly different designs in two joined sections, and one section is joined upside down.[21] With regard to balustrades as well as columns, some joined elements also vary markedly in their degree of weathering or atmospheric soiling, indicating that they were likely originally located in different areas of the semi-outdoor spaces and therefore had different levels of exposure to water and pollution.

Other elements that appear in the historical images are unaccounted for today, including two balusters and features around windows and doors. Exactly which elements were part of the dismantled group purchased by Costa in 1925 is not known because Byne might not have rendered every element in the duo's possession when he provided his sketches to Hearst. Costa did prepare an inventory of the elements, however, or at least fifty-one crates of them prior to their shipment from Mallorca in June 1929. His notes indicate that there were "five

{55}
Mallorcan gallery balustrade, consisting of four balusters originating from Can Ayamans, installed in the former Princeton University Art Museum

complete carved columns; three boxes with 'engraved column bases'; nine boxes with pieces of 'Gothic gallery railing'; two carved split columns and four half-columns carved to fit against a wall; one carved column base and two half 'carved column bases or plinths'; three column capitals; seven bases; window frames and four capitals; two additional half-columns in pieces and a considerable number of fragments of molding and plinth."[22] Of this list, the "nine boxes with pieces of 'Gothic gallery railing'" likely correspond to the balustrades and not the stairway, as the late fifteenth- to early sixteenth-century stair elements were still being restored by Sacanell at the time of this shipment.[23] The overall weight of these crates was documented to be 6,310 kilograms (13,911 pounds), which is far less than the estimated weight of the entire architectural composition today but roughly matches the estimated weight of the gallery elements alone, suggesting that this group of crates consisted largely or solely of elements from Can Ayamans.[24] Some elements listed in the June 1929 inventory have gone missing since leaving Mallorca (including window frames and some gallery elements), yet most are still included in the group at Princeton today.[25]

In contrast to the extensive documentation that exists regarding the parts of the architectural composition originating from Can Ayamans, information related to the stairway elements is significantly more limited. The original location of these elements, which include eight separately carved panels and multiple railing elements that fit together to form the overall run, is not known. They have been linked to a house on Carrer de l'Aigua on the basis of a drawing Byne published in his and Mildred Stapley's *Majorcan Houses and Gardens* in 1928. Three panels of the staircase are rendered above the caption "Calle del Agua," the street name in Castilian rather than Catalan (see fig. 8).[26] Of these three panels, the central one closely corresponds to a stairway panel now at Princeton, identifiable by its circular tracery, inscribed banderoles, and prominent cracks along its outer edges, which have since been repaired and stabilized {56}. The panels in the first and third positions in the drawing are similar to other panels in the group but not an exact match. This does not mean, however, that they are unrelated, as Byne frequently approximated details in his renderings. Although the staircase's connection to Carrer de l'Aigua is not yet fully understood, researchers have noted that it might have originated from a house on this street that was once owned by the Nogués family. This house was demolished by the 1920s, when part of Carrer de l'Aigua disappeared during the renovation of Carrer de

{56}
A stairway panel presumed to originate from Carrer de l'Aigua. Left: the panel rendered in 1928 by Arthur Byne in *Majorcan Houses and Gardens*; right: the panel installed in the Princeton University Art Museum in 2025. Arrows indicate cracks that have been stabilized during previous campaigns of repair

Jaume III. Costa also had a documented association with Carrer de l'Aigua, as he purchased a ceiling from a house on this street during the same period.[27]

Byne rendered this stairway in two of his 1929 drawings for Hearst: once on its own (see fig. 43) and then superimposed into a setting that resembles the published historical images of the inner patio of Can Ayamans (see fig. 42). This patio did once have a decorative stairway, but it ran in the opposite direction to the stairway acquired by Costa. It would have been impossible to install the Carrer de l'Aigua stairway in the way Byne renders it in the latter drawing because its panels are decorated on only one side and therefore can only be installed with the decorated side facing outward. Although the current whereabouts of the stairway in the inner patio of Can Ayamans are unknown, it is certainly not the stairway included with the elements now in Princeton. The stairway now in Princeton does not appear to have originated from the first patio of Can Ayamans either; although there are stairs in this patio that run in the correct direction, late nineteenth-century photographs show the patio-facing side of these stairs to be lined with a solid wall (see figs. 47, 48; the stairway is not visible but is accessed through the doorway on the right in the photographs).

Letters between Byne and Costa contain further evidence that the stairway included with the ensemble was not from Can Ayamans. On May 10, 1929, Byne wrote to Costa, responding to his "two newly dated letters stating the progress made to date with the stones of the stairs; I am glad that 5 whole sections have come out.... As soon as you have all the stones on the floor of the packing room, please let me know. I have to prepare some drawings and at the same time see if it is feasible to combine the stones of the stairs that Sacanell is fixing with those of the patio."[28] The overall ensemble had already been sold to Hearst approximately one month before this letter was written. The elements did not arrive in New York until September 1929, and Byne's final renderings weren't completed until October 1929.[29] In addition to originating from separate locations, the gallery elements of the Can Ayamans patio were dismantled in the late nineteenth century, while the stairway elements were dismantled in or around 1929. In the 1960s Costa did not mention sourcing the stairway from a second location while recalling the sale of the elements from Can Ayamans, and only the Can Ayamans stairway is illustrated in Ripoll's publication.[30] It is understandable, however, that he might not have remembered these details more than thirty years after the sale.

Interestingly, eight square limestone panels attributed to Can Ayamans in the collection of the Museu de Mallorca contain tracery that closely resembles the tracery of the stairway presumed to be from Carrer de l'Aigua. Although this prompts consideration of the possibility that the stairway acquired by Costa and Byne could have originated from Can Ayamans, this is not likely. The attribution of the Museu de Mallorca panels has been questioned in recent decades, but if they are indeed from Can Ayamans, the similarities in design could also be coincidental.[31] The same style of tracery is also present in other regional examples of fifteenth-century architecture, including the stairways of Can Oleo and Can Puigserver. The latter no longer stands but was drawn by Rafael de Ysasi in 1908 {57} {58}.[32]

Although details of the stairway's specific origins are scarce, photographic documentation and other visual evidence suggest that it, too, underwent modifications after its removal from its initial context, much like the elements from Can Ayamans. At least one undated photograph from what is likely the era of Sacanell's restoration shows the stairway mounted in an outdoor or semi-outdoor setting that is partly obscured in the foreground by a pulley and a scaffold.[33] Notably, of the five panels that are visible in the frame, all are arranged in an order that differs from that shown in Byne's 1929 drawing (see fig. 43). The arrangement captured in the drawing remained throughout the twentieth century and is the order in which they are installed today. Byne noted at the top of this drawing that the stairway is rendered in a "corrected form," further indicating that a reordering of the panels occurred while the elements were still in his and Costa's possession.

{57}
Rafael de Ysasi (1862–1948; born London, United Kingdom; died Palma de Mallorca, Spain), drawing of a stairway of Can Puigserver, 1908

{58}
Rafael de Ysasi, drawing of a stairway of Can Puigserver, 1908

He labeled the panels from bottom to top using Roman numerals; today the carved numerals "vi" and "vii" are visible on the bottom edges of the panels located, respectively, in the sixth and seventh positions from the bottom of the run, and they likely date to the era of Sacanell's restoration {59}. Presumably there are carved Roman numerals on other panels as well, but all the other bottom edges are now obscured by mortar or other restoration materials that were applied during previous twentieth-century installation campaigns.

Physical evidence also indicates a rearrangement of the panels. In many instances the panels that are now adjacent to one another contain entirely different weathering patterns, suggesting that they must have spent vastly different amounts of time exposed to outdoor elements, similar to what has been observed on the columns and balustrades (see p. 79). There were multiple attempts during the twentieth century to make these differences less noticeable; limewashes, skim coats, and paints were noted in 2023 that are also visible on elements originating from Can Ayamans.[34] This indicates they were applied after the elements from the two different locations were combined and likely during more than one installation campaign. These materials were significantly reduced during conservation treatment from 2023 to 2025.[35] Additionally, a large rectangular fill at the base of one panel, now located at the bottom of the run, suggests that it

{59}
A Roman numeral vii that likely dates to the era of Sacanell's restoration carved on the bottom edge of a Mallorcan stairway panel

could have once been located either at the top of the run or at a landing, rather than adjacent to another panel.

Although the original arrangement of the panels (or even whether the run might have included more than eight panels) has not yet been determined, some clues might lie in further study of the medieval inscription, written in a dialect of Catalan. The inscription, the source of which is currently unknown, has been translated in recent years as a prayer begging for the Lord's mercy.[36] As noted, the panel order rendered by Byne in 1929 (see fig. 43) is still preserved in the current installation, and from top to bottom the inscription reads:

[...] OREN HOITS	*they were heard*
DELLS SAN [...] S PA	*by the holy Apostolic [fathers]*
E CANTA SON MAL	*and he sings his misfortunes*
DONCEL QVE BALL	*for he who dances*
TRARA LO MAGNAN	*will be brought by the magnanimous*
SENYOR DEMOS	*our Father*
[...] S QVINSTE	*who possesses us*
[...] AR [...] S MORTS	*even now after our death*
NO LOAN ATV SENIOR	*They do not praise you, Lord*
NE LOS HOMENS	*not those men*
QUI D [...] N ENINFERN	*who descend into Hell*
[...] OM [...] A PER	*[Not even] [those] [lost] [men]?*
POR QUILS NARAME	*For all those who do not love him (the Lord)*
SIS FARA ANOS DE	*He will make us out of*
RES LA DINS [...] OS	*Spirit*
LIMS VENC LOSEN	*in order to triumph in the final judgment*[37]

In more recent analysis of the inscription, possibilities for alternative interpretation of some passages were also noted. For example, "RES LA DINS" could mean "There is nothing inside there" (res allà dins), rather than "Spirit." And if read phonetically, "DONCEL QVE BALL" is closer to "from a heaven that descends/from a heaven he descends" (d'un cel que [da] vall [a]).[38]

It is not known how the order of the panels was determined during Sacanell's restoration in the 1920s. Those involved in these decisions might not have been able to read the text or understand its meaning. In his 1929 drawing for Hearst, Byne made little effort to render the inscriptions, despite rendering the circular tracery of each panel in great detail. Instead of the true lettering, scrolls around the tracery are filled with strings of letters or arbitrary Latin or English phrases like "ABCDEFGHIJ" or "OMNIA OPUS." Identifying the source of the text is a worthy topic of further research and may help clarify how the panels were originally configured.

The architectural composition includes two other elements of undetermined Mallorcan origin: a carved stone grotesque with hybrid features of both a dragon and a dog {60} (see also p. 86) and an associated newel post. These elements were included in the group assembled by Costa and Byne and rendered in two of the drawings Byne made for Hearst in 1929; their original location is not clear, however. They might have come from Can Ayamans or the unnamed house on Carrer de l'Aigua, but they also could have originated from a different location entirely. In historical photographs and illustrations of the inner Can Ayamans patio from the nineteenth century, grotesques are visible on the stairway's lower newel posts, but it is unclear if either is the one that is now at Princeton (see figs. 1, 49–51). The post itself does not match.

Through examination of all the individual elements today, as well as a comparison of all known associated images dating to before and after the stairway and gallery elements were combined, it is evident that the restoration undertaken in Mallorca during the 1920s to create a cohesive architectural composition for sale was extensive. By the time the stairway and gallery left the island in 1929, they had been modified and recombined in ways that left them permanently altered. As they changed hands during the twentieth century and the

{60}
Carved newel-post topper of a grotesque with hybrid features of a dragon and a dog

connections to their original locations became blurred, these changes also made them difficult to identify. For this reason the elements from Can Ayamans were considered by scholars to be lost for many years, even though they had been on view in the United States for decades.

Early Years in the United States, 1929–55

In 1929 Byne sold the architectural composition to William Randolph Hearst, who initially intended to install the elements in a house he planned to build in Los Angeles. As Letvin discusses in her essay in this volume, he later considered displaying them in one or more buildings at his growing estate in San Simeon, California, known as La Cuesta Encantada. As architectural plans evolved and budgets tightened over the following years, however, the elements were never installed.

While in Hearst's possession, the elements likely never left his storage warehouse in the Bronx, New York. Like many objects in Hearst's vast architectural holdings, the ensemble was acquired with enthusiasm but ultimately sidelined amid shifting plans and budgets. In inventory records maintained by the International Studio Art Corporation, the elements were listed as "The Majorcan Patio and Stairway from Palma de Majorca, Spain—Dating from the XVI Century" and described as "Consisting of two Arcaded Galleries with carved Parapet, two stone windows, a Gothic stone stair parapet, newel post and several perforated panels of the landing."[39] Further details regarding their appearance and condition were not documented, and no photographs are known to survive. In 1929 Byne mentioned enclosing at least three photographs of the elements in correspondence with Morgan just prior to the sale, but these have since been lost.[40]

As outlined by Letvin, Baron Cassel van Doorn likely acquired the architectural composition at Hearst's liquidation sale at Gimbel Brothers in New York in 1941. By 1942 he had begun planning for its installation at his estate in Englewood, New Jersey. Architectural blueprints survive from that year, prepared by two New York City–based contractors involved with the installation: Miller Druck & Co., Inc. {61} {62} and Pizzutello Stone Works, Inc. {63}.[41]

In Englewood the elements were installed outdoors. The installation included a selection of major architectural components, arranged to form a unified composition that included four full columns, four full column bases, two half (formerly engaged) columns, two half (formerly engaged) column bases, eighteen balusters (arranged in multiple balustrades) with associated railing, all eight panels of the

{61}
Blueprint related to the Mallorcan stairway and gallery's 1942 installation at Jevington Manor, Englewood, New Jersey. Prepared by Miller Druck & Co., Inc. Princeton University Art Museum, Curatorial Files

{62}
Blueprint related to the Mallorcan stairway and gallery's 1942 installation at Jevington Manor, Englewood, New Jersey. Prepared by Miller Druck & Co., Inc. Princeton University Art Museum, Curatorial Files

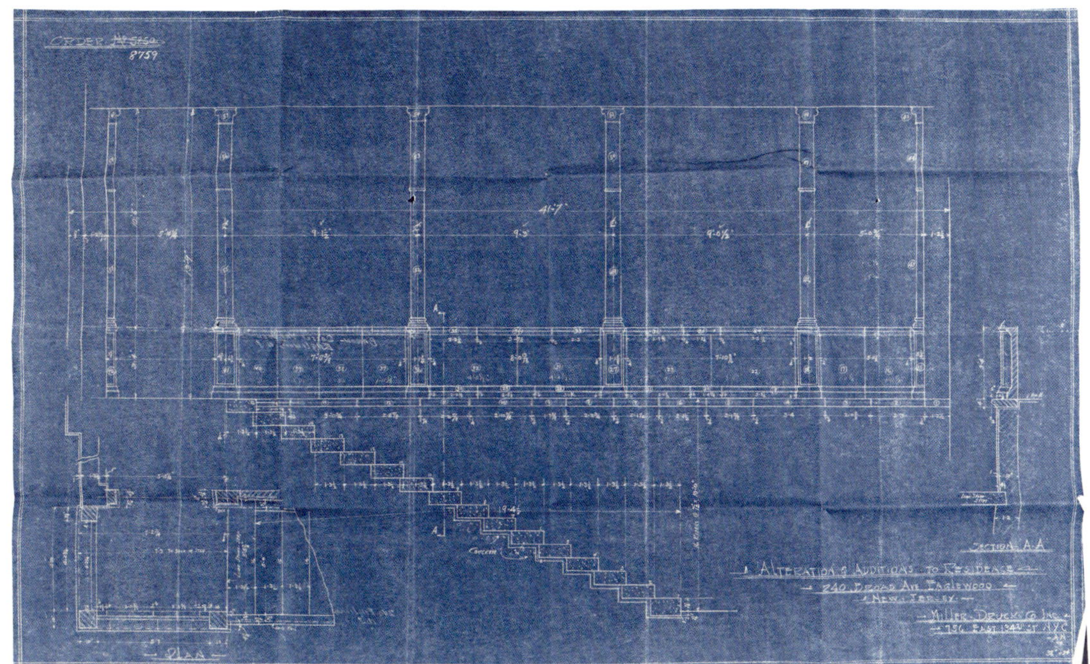
ORDER No
8759
SECTION A-A
ALTERATION & ADDITIONS TO RESIDENCE
240 BROAD AVE ENGLEWOOD
NEW JERSEY
Miller-Druck Co Inc.
PLAN

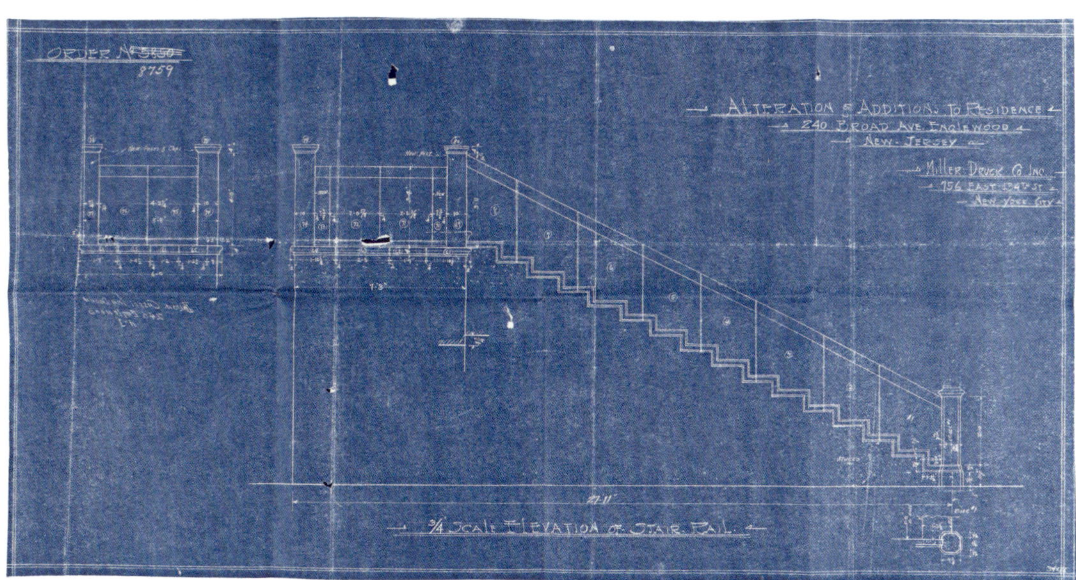
ORDER No
8759
ALTERATION & ADDITIONS TO RESIDENCE
240 BROAD AVE ENGLEWOOD
NEW JERSEY
Miller-Druck Co Inc.
NEW YORK CITY
3/4 SCALE ELEVATION OF STAIR RAIL

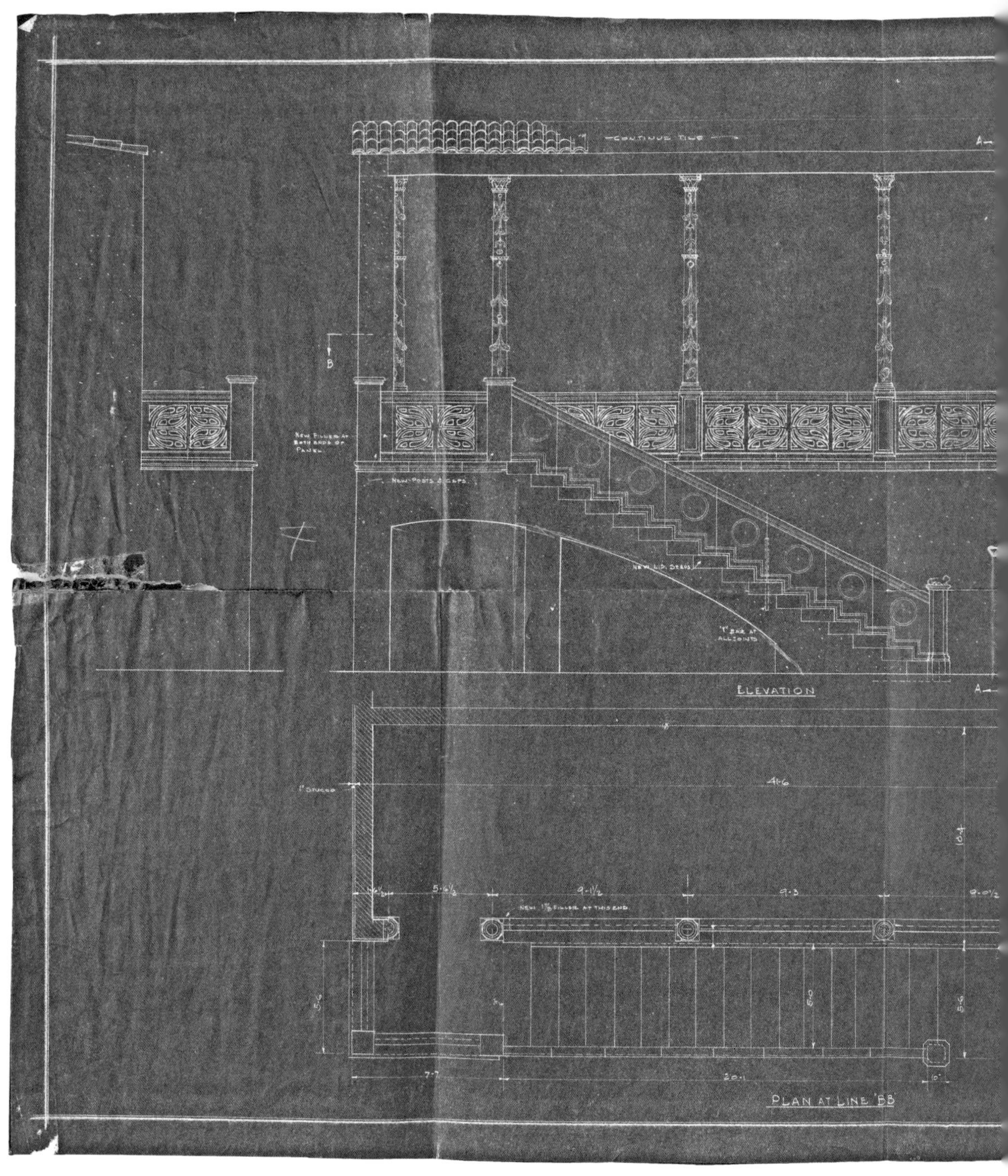
CONTINUE TILE
NEW FILLER AT BOTH ENDS OF PANEL
NEW POSTS & CAPS
NEW U.D. STEPS
ELEVATION
1" STUCCO
4'-6
9-1/2
9-3
NEW 1½ FILLER AT THIS END
7-7
20-1
PLAN AT LINE 'BB'

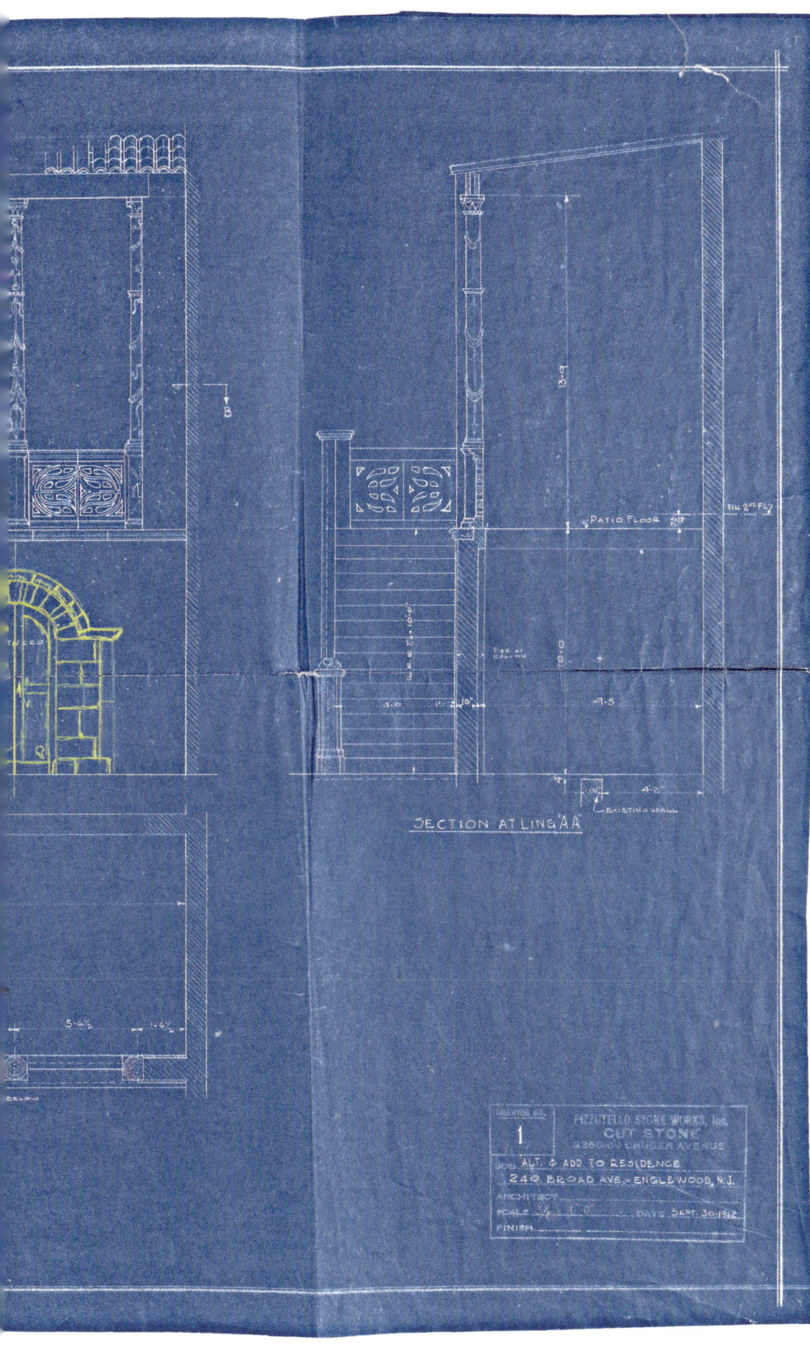

{63}
Blueprint related to the Mallorcan stairway and gallery's 1942 installation at Jevington Manor, Englewood, New Jersey. Prepared by Pizzutello Stone Works, Inc. Princeton University Art Museum, Curatorial Files

stairs with associated railing, and three newel posts (two with flat toppers and one with the grotesque) (see fig. 31). The balustrades and columns were installed on the second level as one single gallery rather than as two galleries, as rendered by Byne; balusters were installed in groups of either two or four, and central columns were evenly spaced. The stairway ran from the ground level to the second level, and its panels were installed in the same order in which they appeared in Byne's drawings from 1929 (see figs. 42, 43). This reconfiguration, dictated by the spatial constraints and aesthetic choices of the Englewood estate, marked the first time the elements were reassembled as a coherent architectural feature, albeit one divorced from their historical context.

Notably, photographs of the Cassel van Doorn composition in Englewood from the 1940s or early 1950s do not include all the elements that were rendered by Byne in 1929 or listed in Costa's partial inventory from that year. For example, Costa's inventory lists window elements and additional column elements that are unaccounted for in the Englewood composition. Byne's renderings also show twenty baluster elements, yet the Englewood composition included only eighteen. A detailed inventory of the elements was not documented either by the International Studio Art Corporation or by Baron Cassel van Doorn around the point of sale, so it is not clear if every element transferred from Byne to Hearst in 1929 was also transferred to Cassel van Doorn in the early 1940s. It is possible that some elements were installed in another area of the Cassel van Doorn residence, though that is unlikely, as none are visible in the many surviving photographs from the 1940s and 1950s of the interior and exterior of the house. Today the elements that are not included in photographs of the Englewood composition are also not part of the group in Princeton. Moving large-scale architectural ensembles from one location to another introduces a heightened risk of loss. In the case of the stairway and gallery from Mallorca, elements appear to have gone missing each time they changed hands.

Evidence suggests that the Cassel van Doorns did indeed once have the window elements that are now lost. Although these elements are not included in photographs from Englewood or rendered in the architectural blueprints from 1942, there is a small, loose sketch of a window on the back of one blueprint by Pizzutello Stone Works {64}.[42] The general shape and noted dimensions of the window in this sketch are consistent with windows drawn by Byne in 1929: one sketched above a note that reads, "2 windows like this" (see fig. 44),

{64}
Sketch of now-lost window elements on the back of the 1942 blueprint prepared by Pizzutello Stone Works, Inc. Princeton University Art Museum, Curatorial Files

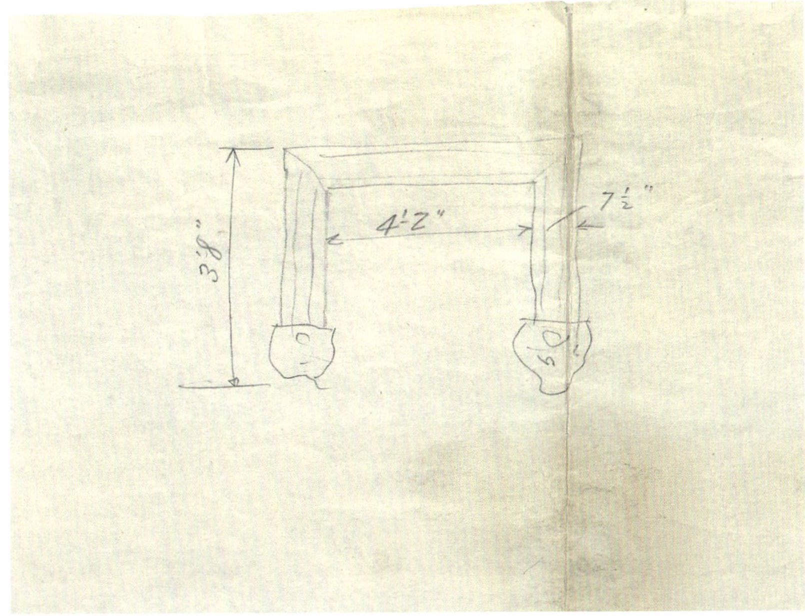

and another above a note that reads, "TWO WINDOW HEADS LIKE THIS" (see fig. 45).

New limestone elements were also created for the Englewood installation to complete the composition, including at least two newel posts for the landing at the top of the stairs; in Pizzutello's 1942 blueprint, there is a note beneath these elements that reads, "NEW POSTS & CAPS." Historical elements were also modified. A balustrade section consisting of two joined baluster elements was extended with stone fills at either end—in the same blueprint a note reads, "NEW FILLERS AT BOTH ENDS OF PANEL."[43] All modifications and additions appear to have been made to ensure that the elements would fit into the arrangement determined for this specific location, which was different than the arrangement proposed by Byne decades earlier. These additions were stylistically compatible with the historical fragments but not clearly differentiated, raising questions about authorship and authenticity that later complicated efforts to identify the original elements.

The elements were installed by 1944 and remained outdoors at the Cassel van Doorn estate for approximately a decade. After the baron died in 1952, the baroness sold the Englewood property and dispersed the collection, donating the Mallorcan stairway and gallery elements and other architectural works of art to the Princeton University Art Museum in 1955.[44]

Arrival at Princeton and Installation in the Former Museum Building, 1955–66

When the elements first arrived at Princeton, there was no immediate plan to display them, so they were delivered to the basement of Nassau Hall for long-term storage.[45] This building, the oldest on Princeton University's campus, briefly served as the US Capitol during the American Revolutionary War and is now home to the offices of the University's president. The Museum's 1955 accession card includes a description of the elements that closely matches the brief description in Hearst's records, and it is not clear whether the Museum took a formal inventory of elements at this time (see fig. 3).[46] The decade-long hiatus between acquisition and eventual installation in 1965 not only delayed curatorial assessment but also contributed to significant gaps in documentation and institutional memory surrounding the ensemble.

The elements were installed in the Museum's gallery of medieval art, where they remained from 1965 until 2021. The composition was markedly different from the Cassel van Doorn configuration. The columns and balustrades were arranged in two galleries, rather than one: Half of the columns and balustrades were installed on the north side of the gallery, extending from the west wall toward the center of the gallery, and half were installed on the south side of the gallery, extending from the east wall toward the center of the gallery {65}. The stairway elements were installed on both sides of the stairs leading to the works on paper study room on the third floor: Four panels lined the left side of the stairs, and four panels lined the right side of the stairs {66} (see also fig. 2). Modern stair treads were added to make the stairway functional. The overall composition of the elements was altered only once, in 2010, in response to a construction project that entailed shifting the gallery elements nearest to the Museum's study room from the east wall to the west wall {67}. The placement of two columns and their associated bases and capitals was also changed.[47] Today only limited information exists in the Museum's files regarding the 1965 installation, and details about how decisions were made regarding the arrangement of the composition are lacking. While preparing for the ensemble's 2025 installation, however, we were able to piece together additional information from the University's archives.

In 1959 Princeton University President Robert F. Goheen began a three-year campaign to raise $53 million for the University, in a drive for a "stronger Princeton" that would support new construction projects, renovations, endowment funds for teaching and research, and working capital.[48] Included in these projects was an expansion of the

{65}
Mallorcan stairway and gallery, installed in the Princeton University Art Museum

{66}
Mallorcan stairway leading to the works on paper study room in the Princeton University Art Museum

{67}
The Mallorcan gallery elements installed nearest to the stairway were shifted from the east wall to the west wall in 2010

Museum. At the time collections were displayed in a building designed in 1890 by Arthur Page Brown (1859–1896), while the Department of Art & Archaeology and Marquand Library were housed in the connected McCormick Hall, which was a 1923 expansion designed by Ralph Adams Cram (1863–1942). Updated spaces had long been needed, but insufficient funding and indecision in planning caused delays in growth throughout the 1940s and 1950s. The architectural firm Steinmann, Cain & White (later Steinmann & Cain) was selected in 1959 to design a new building. The principal designer for the project was Walker O. Cain (Graduate School Class of 1940), and the supervising architect was John G. Faron (Class of 1935, Graduate School Class of 1939). Final designs were approved by Goheen and the Trustees of Princeton University in 1962, and by the beginning of 1964 bids for construction work on the new Museum had been accepted and building plans had been finalized. The general contractor was Rheinstein Construction Company, a firm based in New York City and owned by Alfred Rheinstein (Class of 1911). Severud-Elstat-Krueger Associates served as structural engineers, while Meyer, Strong, and Jones served as mechanical engineers.[49]

The Museum was also undergoing changes in leadership at this time. Ernest T. DeWald (Graduate School Class of 1914, 1916), who had served as director of the Museum since 1946, was involved in advocacy, fundraising, and initial planning for the new building until his retirement in 1960. He was succeeded by Patrick J. Kelleher (Graduate School Class of 1942, 1947), who led the Museum through the construction and installation phases of the project. It was decided during planning that many large architectural stone objects donated by Baroness Cassel van Doorn in 1955 would be incorporated into the design of the new building. This group of works included not only the stairway and gallery elements from Mallorca but also several architectural elements from France (see Letvin's essay in this volume): a fifteenth-century window from Vaucluse (see fig. 30), a fifteenth-century window from Rozérieulles (Moselle), and three doorways. Carl Otto Kretzschmar von Kienbusch (Class of 1906), a prominent collector and longtime Museum adviser, played a key role in securing the donation from the baroness. An advocate for expanding Princeton's collections, Kienbusch facilitated discussions between the baroness and Museum Director Ernest DeWald after the baron's death in 1952.[50] His influence helped persuade the baroness to donate these objects to Princeton, thus ensuring their long-term preservation and future display.

To prepare for installation of the architectural elements in the 1960s, Steinmann & Cain borrowed the relevant object files from the Museum. A handwritten note from Faron indicates that the architects returned the file for the stairway and gallery elements from Mallorca in April 1962, with the exception of five documents that were retained for further study: one blueprint from 1942 (associated with the installation at the Cassel van Doorns' estate) and four photographic reproductions (presumably of the four drawings Arthur Byne prepared for William Randolph Hearst in October 1929).[51] Although Steinmann & Cain had access to documents related to two previous configurations, they chose a different arrangement of the elements for the new Museum. Little is known about how this decision was made, and planning renderings prepared by the architects have since been lost.

Throughout planning and construction of the new building, progress meetings were held every two weeks that included the architects, representatives from the Museum and the University, and all necessary contractors. Minutes were recorded by Steinmann & Cain during each meeting and distributed to all participants afterward.[52] Today these records serve as resources for understanding multiple aspects of the complex project, in particular how contracts were organized, how construction timelines were structured, and how teams collaborated to advance the work.

By early 1963 the elements from Mallorca had been flagged by Steinmann & Cain as needing special resources to install. According to meeting notes from February 14 of that year: "The Architects pointed out that construction costs do not include the installation of exhibits. They suggested that the administration be made aware of this fact, noting that the installation of the Spanish Stair, nymphaeum [y1940-437], and Antioch mosaics [including y1965-217 and y1965-216, among others] will certainly involve considerable cost."[53] In the following months, the Rheinstein Construction Company's initial contract for construction of the new building was expanded to include installation of the Museum's oversize and embedded collection objects as well. These included the gifts from the baroness as well as archaeological mosaics and other architectural features. In July 1963 the elements from Mallorca were moved from the basement of Nassau Hall to room 106 of McCormick Hall, a "Big Study Room" where they could be uncrated and then stored with other large objects in advance of installation.[54]

By the end of 1963 concerns began to develop over the safety of objects stored at the construction site. In December, Richard Stillwell, professor of archaeology and architectural history in the Department of Art & Archaeology, wrote to R.L. Johnstone of the University's Office of Physical Planning, who was overseeing construction: "Recently it appears that some of the students from the School of Architecture have been 'salvaging' things. You will have a memorandum from Joe [i.e., Patrick J.] Kelleher on this since the main part of what is left in McCormick is the Museum's concern. I am, however, anxious about what might happen if an irresponsible group went in, and let us say, threw a party on the top floor of the building, with possible risk of fire, or lesser damage."[55]

Alfred Rheinstein also wrote to Faron a few weeks later, in February 1964, to request the University perform a condition assessment and inventory of the objects. He also proposed building a protective enclosure.[56] By March an inventory was undertaken by Frances Follin Jones, the Museum's curator of collections. Jones recorded descriptions of each object and further documented their appearance in a series of annotated black-and-white photographs {68}. In her entry for the elements from Mallorca, the group is listed as "Carved limestone stairway and loggia; Spanish." She listed a number of components:

> Newel post, animal on top.
> 8 panels of balustrade for stairway, each with openwork medallion in center.
> 6 slender rectangular pedestals with round columns above. (One column has its capital.)
> 3 rectangular pedestals.
> 10 openwork intercolumnar grilles for balustrades of loggia, in 13 sections (one badly broken).
> 19 pieces of capping stone for balustrades.[57]

Although only one capital is listed, the Museum had a total of six in its possession (four full, two half); the other five had been left in the basement of Nassau Hall but were moved to McCormick Hall later that year.[58] The "3 rectangular pedestals" are likely all posts that were created in the 1940s for the Englewood installation. The "10 openwork intercolumnar grilles for balustrades of loggia" are the eighteen baluster elements, just counted by Jones in different groupings.

In addition to the security challenges on the construction site, weather created obstacles. In December 1964 a representative from Frommeyer & Company, Rheinstein's subcontractor for building masonry, joined the bimonthly progress meeting to discuss his team's

{68}
Mallorcan stairway and gallery elements, in "Objects Stored in 'Big Study Room,' McCormick Hall, Photographed in February, 1964," prepared by Frances Follin Jones. Princeton University Library. Department of Special Collections

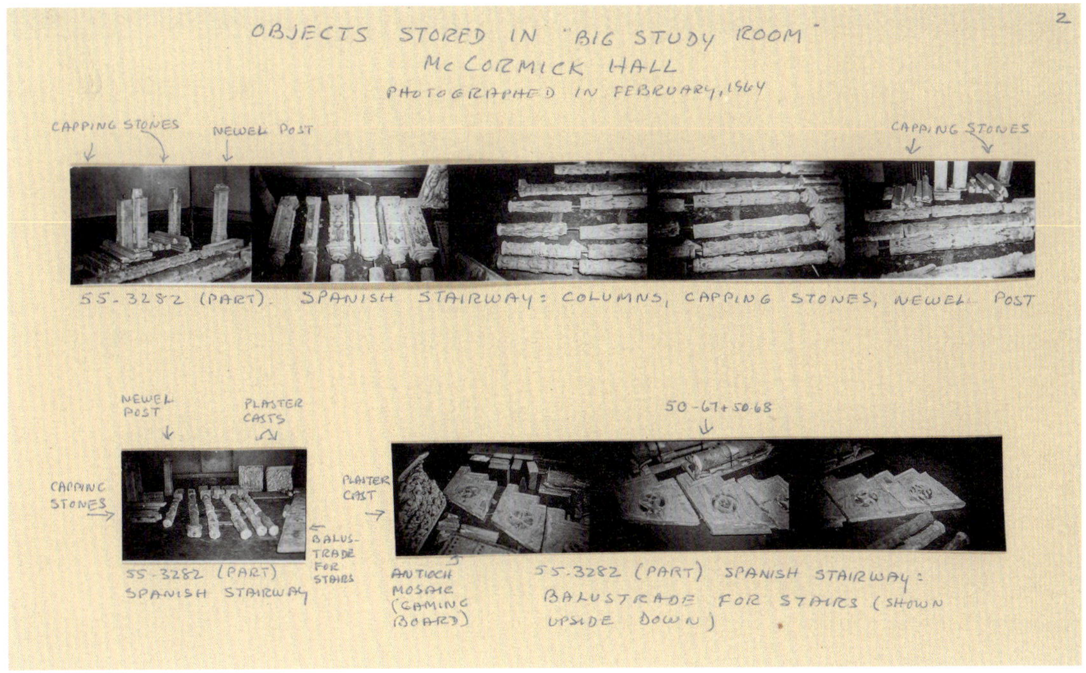

on-site requirements for winter. He noted that mortar would not set below the temperature of twenty-eight degrees Fahrenheit.[59] Although Rheinstein was urged by both the University and the architects to implement measures that would support these working conditions, it was so cold inside the building by late January that the masons were unable to work, and contractors from both Rheinstein's team and Middlesex Sheet Metal (Rheinstein's contractor for metalwork) were threatening to walk off the job.[60]

The low temperatures would also have impacted the installation timelines for the architectural elements from the collections. As with the rest of the building, mortar was used during pointing—the process of filling and sealing joins between stones. The Rheinstein Construction Company began installing the stairway and gallery elements from Mallorca in the medieval gallery sometime after January 1965.[61] The company's work involved collaboration with other contractors, but most names and contributions were not documented. The University hired L. Stanley Reed of nearby West Windsor, New Jersey, for masonry needs on collection objects in the European and ancient Mediterranean galleries, and though the details of his work were only sparsely documented, it is likely he completed masonry work on the elements from Mallorca as well.[62]

At least one campaign of structural and aesthetic intervention occurred on the stairway and gallery in early 1965, although the full scope of this work is unclear and the specifics were not documented. Multiple materials from twentieth-century campaigns of repair and installation were noted during the 2023–25 conservation treatment, but it was not always possible to determine when they might have been applied, as many of the tools and materials used to repair and install stone elements remained generally consistent through the twentieth century.[63] Some of the toning materials closely resembled those on other architectural objects that had been installed in the Museum's medieval gallery in the 1960s, however, including an Italian stone doorway (y1950-22) that was not part of the group of objects donated by the baroness.[64] Moreover, in Jones's 1964 black-and-white inventory photographs of the dismantled group of elements in McCormick Hall's "Big Study Room" (see fig. 68), many elements appear significantly more soiled than in photographs taken soon after their 1965 installation. The layers of toning that were applied in 1965, as well as other layers believed to have been applied after the elements were removed from their original settings in Mallorca and before they reached Princeton, were significantly reduced during the 2023–25 conservation treatment. While likely intended to unify the ensemble visually, these interventions also masked the distinctions between elements of different origin and condition. As a result, the restored composition conveyed a false sense of historical coherence, complicating efforts to interpret the ensemble's true formation.

Aside from aesthetic restoration, structural repair was also performed during the 1965 installation. There are cracks and losses visible in Jones's 1964 inventory photographs that appear patched and filled in photographs taken soon after these elements were installed in the Museum. Additionally, all baluster elements were installed intact, despite the note about a badly broken balustrade in Jones's 1964 inventory. Some or all of this structural repair work was performed by the Rheinstein Construction Company, though this appears to have been done reluctantly. In 1965 Alfred Rheinstein wrote to Faron to note that his team had spent significant time and resources performing restoration-related tasks that he believed were outside the scope of their contract:

> Following is a summary of the charges we have had to date for work not included in our price to set the permanent exhibit, including the cost of removing mortar from joints, which item you have questioned. Our work is limited to setting and does not include restoration. We feel that removal of mortar from an old piece of stone preparatory to setting it in place is as much of a job of restoration, for which we are renumerated [*sic*], as is filling a piece of splayed stone, and was not figured by us in our estimate of $8,000. We do not wish to appear picayune but this work is costing a great deal of money in terms of direct labor as well as the time involved by superintendents, Officers' time and other overhead costs.[65]

Though specific Museum collection objects are not mentioned in this complaint, the recorded minutes from the next bimonthly progress meeting confirm that the restoration work did indeed include the elements from Mallorca. Faron notes, "One T&M [Time & Materials] slip, totaling 41 hours ... included work involved in patching of balustrades for the Spanish Stair and the Venetian Door [y1950-22]."[66] It is unclear who asked Rheinstein's team to perform this work, but a handwritten note in the margin of Rheinstein's letter of complaint, presumably from Faron, reads, "Not Reed?," indicating that Steinmann & Cain may have considered some of the restoration work billed by Rheinstein to instead have been among the responsibilities assigned to mason L. Stanley Reed.[67] It is possible that Reed worked on other repairs as well.

In March 1965 it was noted in bimonthly meeting minutes that a "lintel" from the group of elements was not on the job site and therefore could not be installed above the door to the third-floor works on paper study room.[68] In all known historical inventories, a lintel is never noted. Steinmann & Cain might, however, have used this term to describe one of the two windows from Can Ayamans that were once included with the group yet are now lost. These windows are not believed to have been among the elements donated by the baroness, but the architects likely assumed them to be in the Museum's possession because the elements were both listed on the Museum's 1955 accession card and rendered in Byne's 1929 drawings that were studied during planning. By April 1965, after a month of searching, Faron reported that all efforts to locate the missing "lintel" had been unsuccessful, and the installation proceeded without it.[69]

All Mallorcan stairway and gallery elements installed outdoors at the estate in Englewood were installed in the Museum in 1965 with the exception of one newel post. This post was rendered by Byne in 1929 (see figs. 42, 43) and was documented and photographed during Jones's March 1964 inventory of objects stored in McCormick Hall, but it was not installed in the medieval gallery in 1965 because it had been stolen from the jobsite. Thus, the concerns regarding safety and security on the construction site were valid. In October 1965, months after the rest of the elements had already been installed, Kelleher noted in a letter to John Moran, assistant general manager in the Department of Physical Facilities and Properties, that the newel post had been recently recovered from an undergraduate dormitory and needed to be "reset."[70] Kelleher did not specify if the newel-post topper containing the grotesque was also included in this theft. The topper was installed, however, while the post itself was returned to storage and replaced with a plain post from the group of elements that was fabricated in the 1940s for the Englewood installation. The architectural composition was in place by the end of 1965, and installation of the collections continued into the following year.

Preparing for a New Building, 2018–25

The Museum's decision in 2018 to construct a new building created both a logistical challenge and an interpretive opportunity for the Mallorcan stairway and gallery. This new building, which would be located on the same site as the Steinmann & Cain building, in the center of Princeton University's campus, would include more gallery space to display the Museum's collections, multiple classrooms to support object-based learning, and a state-of-the-art two-story conservation studio. Sir David Adjaye of Adjaye Associates was selected as project architect, with Cooper Robertson serving as executive architects.[71]

The former building was scheduled for demolition in 2021. Several thousand objects, including the elements from Mallorca, were packed and transported to temporary storage. Dozens of architectural works and archaeological mosaics had been embedded in the former building since the 1960s, and the removal of these items was acutely challenging because of their large size, specific logistical needs, and particular equipment requirements. Often, as was the case with the stairway and gallery elements, only limited documentation survived from their installation decades ago. In some instances previous gallery renovation campaigns had also changed surrounding spaces in ways that made embedded objects difficult to locate. For example, the fourteenth-century stone doorway from France (y1955-3284), also donated by Baroness Cassel van Doorn, was found completely obscured behind a gallery wall, and a third-century mosaic from Antioch (y1965-215) had to be removed from beneath the floor of the Museum's gift shop.

Due to the complex needs associated with the removal of the oversize and embedded works, the Museum contracted a wide network of specialists to assist with the removal process, which continued through the height of the COVID-19 pandemic lockdowns. In 2020 EverGreene Architectural Arts was contracted to oversee the deinstallation of the elements from Mallorca, thus beginning a five-year relationship with the Museum's team. Led by Kelly Caldwell, director of conservation, EverGreene worked closely with the Museum and other subcontractors over multiple weeks to dismantle the composition and pack its elements. In 2021, after all objects were safely in storage, the former building was demolished as preparations for the new building began.

During the early architectural planning stages, it was decided that the stairway and gallery elements from Mallorca would be moved out of the galleries and into a much more prominent location next to the new Grand Stair. They would also be displayed on a long, elevated platform, and visitors would not be able to walk on or through the stairway or gallery. Previously the elements had been installed throughout the Museum's medieval gallery in ways that encouraged visitor interaction: Columns and balustrades had been installed directly on the floor, and stair panels and railings had lined both sides of a public stairway. Over time, however, dark staining accumulated in areas where visitors most often touched the stone. These stains had to be reduced during conservation treatment. For the first time at Princeton, this new configuration would allow the composition to be viewed as a work of art rather than as a functional architectural feature.

Research into the elements' past revealed that the restoration work performed in the 1920s by Miguel Sacanell was so extensive that the elements could no longer be exhibited as they once had in their original contexts. The dismantled elements were recombined in ways that involved mixing and matching components, forming joins where joins never existed, and removing or reducing areas of original stone. In many instances, this work cannot be undone without further alteration of original stone. The 1920s formation of this architectural composition marks an irreversible era of the elements' past.

Modifications continued throughout the twentieth century, particularly as the elements changed hands and were installed in new locations. Hearst kept the stairway and gallery in storage while they were in his possession between 1929 and 1941, so it is not known how he and Morgan might have chosen to display them. When installed in Englewood in the 1940s by Baron Cassel van Doorn, fitting the elements into a preexisting outdoor space involved removal, addition, and reconfiguration. When the elements were first installed at the Museum in 1965, they were once again reconfigured based on aesthetic decisions made by Steinmann & Cain.

By understanding more about the fifteenth- and sixteenth-century origins of the elements and how they have changed throughout the twentieth century, the Museum's staff and the specialists at EverGreene came to realize that the stairway and gallery could not be reassembled in a configuration that resembled their original arrangement or their prior arrangement in the Museum. Nor was that preferred, as previous campaigns of restoration and installation marked significant events in the elements' past. In planning for the Museum's new building in the years leading up to 2025, it was decided that all joins that were created between elements during twentieth-century installations would be left intact, as any join reversals risked further damage to the limestone. Some of these joins and previous structural repairs needed to be stabilized and reinforced.

All surfaces were cleaned to reduce staining and toning layers from the twentieth century, but atmospheric soiling located beneath these layers (which was believed to predate the elements' journey to the United States) was left intact. Additional filling and toning were applied minimally and only where necessary. In the end, the conservation treatment allows visitors to better visualize two important aspects of the composition's history: first, that some elements have been modified or recombined, and second, that the stairway and gallery elements are of different origins.

Architectural decisions had been made for the Entrance Hall area before research into the elements' past had concluded, so there were some limitations in how elements could be spaced and installed in the new setting. The area is not large enough to contain every single element, so it was decided to include twelve of the eighteen balusters and the associated railing, all four full columns and associated column bases and capitals, all eight openwork panels of the stairs with inscriptions, the entire stair railing, two nonoriginal newel posts (one at the top of the stairs, fabricated during the Cassel van Doorn installation in the 1940s, and the other at the base of the stairs, fabricated by EverGreene in 2024), and the grotesque newel-post topper (see fig. 60 and p. 86). The two half columns (and their associated column bases), six balusters (and associated railing), and three newel posts (one from Mallorca and two from the United States) were moved to storage, where they are still accessible to researchers.

Since the ceiling height in the Entrance Hall area is very tall, all elements were installed on a single level rather than across two levels. The display space is also only forty-two inches deep, so it was decided to install the entire run of the stairway against the wall, with gallery elements installed directly in front of it (configured as one long, continuous gallery rather than two separate galleries). The stairway elements are arranged in the order created in the 1920s. This was not the original order in Mallorca, but it is the order that has remained consistent throughout the twentieth century (only with the run split in half for the previous installation at Princeton) and is now the only order possible without further changes to the original stone. The grotesque is installed atop the post at the base of the stairs, and the animal is positioned to look out toward visitors. The columns are spaced evenly between balustrades (arranged 1 full column—4 balusters—1 full column—4 balusters—1 full column—4 balusters—1 full column). Overall, this arrangement most closely matches how the elements were installed in Englewood, just now on one level and with

S
STANDARD

{69}
Installation of the Mallorcan stairway and gallery in the Entrance Hall of the Princeton University Art Museum, fall 2024

{70}
Pointing of joints during the installation of the Mallorcan stairway and gallery, fall 2024

fewer gallery elements. This display is thus not a return to an "original" but a careful acknowledgment of the ensemble's evolving material, interpretive, and institutional histories, bound by the architecture of the current space.

The installation of the stairway and gallery in the Entrance Hall of the new Museum was completed in the fall of 2024, and aesthetic conservation treatment was finalized in summer 2025 {69} {70}. The configuration is the result of recent cross-disciplinary research that has significantly deepened the Museum's understanding of the complex history of the composition's individual elements. Between 2020 and 2025 curators and conservators revisited long-standing questions about these elements' origins, transformations, and past restorations—an inquiry that had not been undertaken since they entered the Museum's collections in 1955. More than just a study of a single architectural composition, this research sheds light on the larger forces that shaped the movement of historical works across borders during the first half of the twentieth century. The ensemble's journey from Mallorca to Princeton mirrors the shifting landscape of art dealing, collecting, and heritage laws in the 1920s and 1930s, when figures such as Arthur Byne and Josep Costa Ferrer played a key role in the transatlantic trade of Spanish architectural works. Conservation efforts were critical in revealing how the elements had been repeatedly altered to fit new spaces and collectors' visions, highlighting the ways in which architectural objects are often not static but continually reshaped over time.

Notes

Introduction

pages 9–24

1. Several individuals contributed to building the Princeton University Art Museum's curatorial file for the Mallorcan stairway and gallery, which in turn shaped our initial encounter with the ensemble and helped us determine new pathways for research. They include Betsy Rosasco, research curator of European painting and sculpture emerita, and Johanna Seasonwein, former Andrew W. Mellon Curatorial Fellow for Academic Programs, who spearheaded research on the Mallorcan patio elements during the 2009–10 renovation of the Museum's gallery of medieval art and collaborated with then Princeton graduate student Enric Mallorquí-Ruscalleda to translate the stairway's inscriptions and begin piecing together its history. In a recent article, Mallorquí-Ruscalleda reflects on his experience working with the Museum and publishes his translation of the stairway's inscriptions. See Enric Mallorquí-Ruscalleda, "From Palma to Princeton: Reconstruction and Translation of the (Lost) Gothic-Renaissance Staircase of Calle del Agua," *Mirabilia Journal* 38, no. 1 (2024): 358–80. Colleagues at Christie's, including William B. Russell Jr., provided the Museum with images of the stairway and gallery installed at the Cassel van Doorn estate in Englewood, New Jersey.

2. A foundational English-language text on Mallorca's medieval history is David Abulafia, *A Mediterranean Emporium: The Catalan Kingdom of Majorca* (Cambridge University Press, 1994).

3. Eduard Riu-Barrera, "Civil Gothic Architecture in Catalonia, Mallorca and Valencia (13th–15th Centuries)," *Catalan Historical Review*, no. 13 (2020): 27–42.

4. Gottfried Kerscher, "Migration of Elements of Islamic Art into Italy from Spain and the Balearic Islands in the Fourteenth Century," in *Crossing Cultures: Conflict, Migration and Convergence; The Proceedings of the 32nd International Congress of the History of Art*, ed. Jaynie Anderson (Melbourne University Publishing, 2009), 588–91; and Doron Bauer, "Islamicate Goods in Gothic Halls: The *Nachleben* of Palma de Mallorca's Islamic Past," in *Artistic and Cultural Dialogues in the Late Medieval Mediterranean*, ed. María Marcos Cobaleda (Palgrave Macmillan, 2021), 99–115.

5. Miquel À. Capellà Galmés and Joan Domenge i Mesquida, "La escalera en los patios señoriales de Palma de Mallorca: Tipología y ornamentación," *LEXICON: Storie e Architettura in Sicilia*, no. 2 (2021): 397–410.

6. Alejandro Sanz de la Torre, "Las casas señoriales de Palma y los viajeros románticos," *Bolletí de la Societat Arqueològica Lul·liana: Revista d'Estudis Històrics*, no. 55 (1999): 389–98.

7. Arthur Byne and Mildred Stapley Byne, *Majorcan Houses and Gardens: A Spanish Island in the Mediterranean* (W. Helburn, 1928), plate 160.

8. The residence has also been referred to as Posada de s'Estorell or Can Pacs-Fuster at other times during its history.

9. The level of Fuster's involvement in the design is not known. See Donald G. Murray and Aina Pascual, *La casa y el tiempo: Interiores señoriales de Palma* (José J. de Olañeta, 1999), 62–63.

10. Mercé Gambús, "L'obra de l'escultor Joan de Salas a Mallorca (1526–1538): Noves aportacions," *Bolletí de la Societat Arqueològica Lul·liana: Revista d'Estudis Històrics*, no. 64 (2008): 261. Gambús writes that Aina Pascual knew of a financial register connecting Felip Fuster with Joan de Salas and suggests the artist may have worked on Can Ayamans.

11. Costa's account of acquiring the dismantled elements from Can Ayamans was published by Luis Ripoll, "Notas sobre unas piedras viejas y su traslado a Norteamérica," *Papeles de Son Armadans*, no. 89 (August 1963): 265–71.

12. José Miguel Merino de Cáceres and María José Martínez Ruiz, "Arthur Byne, Mildred Stapley, José Costa y el patio de la Casa Ayamans (Palma de Mallorca): Detalles de un despojo artístico en el contexto de la promoción turística balear," *Espacio, tiempo y forma* 7, no. 10 (2022): 121–50. While the authors were not aware of the Princeton ensemble, their exhaustive work documenting the assembly, sale, and export of the Ayamans patio and its combination with the stairway likely from the Carrer de l'Aigua—and the business relationship between Byne and Costa—is crucial to understanding how Princeton's gallery and stairway came to be formed and exported to the United States.
13. Richard Kagan, *The Spanish Craze: America's Fascination with the Hispanic World, 1779–1939* (University of Nebraska Press, 2019).
14. Various dates for the purchase have been given, with 1913 as the most common. Olga Raggio, "The Vélez Blanco Patio: An Italian Renaissance Monument from Spain," *Metropolitan Museum of Art Bulletin* 23, no. 4 (December 1964): 141–76, states "shortly before 1913," while Tommaso Mozzati, "The Vélez Blanco Patio and United States–Cuba Relationships in the 1950s," *Metropolitan Museum Journal* 56 (2021): 51–67, gives 1910.
15. Conversations regarding the dismantling of Blumenthal's mansion began in 1943, and the home was demolished in 1945. Under Met Director Francis H. Taylor, the patio was intended to be reconstructed in a new space as part of an ambitious plan for an enlarged museum; between 1948 and 1950, however, when fundraising goals fell short, the building project was curtailed with a focus on modernizing preexisting wings. During that time the Met considered relocating the patio to Washington, DC, or Cuba. Finally, in 1955, the architectural firm Brown, Lawford and Forbes was hired to prepare plans for a new wing for the library. Construction began in 1962, and the patio reconstruction began in August 1963. See the prefatory note by James J. Rorimer, director, in Raggio, "Vélez Blanco Patio," 141, and Mozzati, "Vélez Blanco Patio."
16. Raggio, "Vélez Blanco Patio," 143–45.
17. Mozzati, "Vélez Blanco Patio," 62, citing a 1960 report from Raggio to Rorimer in the European Sculpture and Decorative Arts curatorial files. Indeed, Blumenthal himself had made changes to the patio to incorporate it into his mansion, and it was frequently referred to not as the Vélez Blanco patio but as the Blumenthal patio.

Alexandra Letvin
pages 25–68

1. José Ruiz Mas, "Early Twentieth-Century American Travelers and Art Dealers of the Spanish Artistic and Historical Heritage: Arthur and Mildred Stapley Byne and Their Double Lives as Plunderers and Travel Writers," *Revista de estudios norteamericanos* 27 (2023): 6.
2. Byne lists his place of birth as Philadelphia in the Hispanic Society Members Files, but most contemporaneous news articles about him give his place of birth as Newark, as does his 1919 application for a US passport.
3. "Arthur Byne Dies; Authority on Spanish Art," *New York Herald Tribune*, July 17, 1935, 12A.
4. Stapley frequently used her maiden name, rather than her married name, in publications and correspondence; her maiden name is employed throughout this text. Little is known about her early life beyond what appears in a 1927 article: Helen Fitzgerald, "Tramped from Cape to Cairo: Mildred Stapley Byne, Authority on Spanish Architecture, Has Traversed Length of Dark Continent," *Brooklyn Eagle*, Sunday, April 10, 1927, 93. She also describes the experience of studying as a young woman in Paris in Mildred Stapley, "Is Paris Wise for the Average American Girl?," *Ladies' Home Journal*, April 1906, 16, 54. According to the membership records of the Hispanic Society, she was born in New York in December 1879. Most other sources give her birth year as 1875.
5. Fitzgerald, "Tramped from Cape to Cairo."
6. Mildred Stapley Byne, "Who's Who of Mildred Byne," handwritten undated notes, Society of Woman Geographers Records, Manuscript Division, Library of Congress, Washington, DC, MSS65707 (hereafter cited as SWG), part 1, box 6, folder 3.
7. Richard L. Kagan, *The Spanish Craze: America's Fascination with the Hispanic World, 1779–1939* (University of Nebraska Press, 2019). Kagan offers a comprehensive overview of the most prominent collectors in the chapter "Collectors and Collecting," 230–304. On Sargent, see Sarah Cash, Elaine Kilmurray, and Richard Ormond, *Sargent & Spain*, exh. cat. (National Gallery of Art, Washington, DC, 2022).
8. Ellen Prokop, "'Here One *Feels* Existence': Isabella Stewart Gardner's Spanish Cloister," in *Collecting Spanish Art: Spain's*

Golden Age and America's Gilded Age, ed. José Luis Colomer and Inge Reist (Frick Collection in association with Centro de Estudios Europa Hispánica, and Center for Spain in America, 2012), 97–123. Intent on acquiring *El Jaleo* from its owner, Thomas Jefferson Coolidge, Gardner designed the cloister before successfully persuading Coolidge to give the painting to her.

9. Tommaso Mozzati, "The Vélez Blanco Patio and United States–Cuba Relationships in the 1950s," *Metropolitan Museum Journal* 56 (2021): 51–67. As Kagan notes, Huntington considered the patio, describing it as "a piece of plunder of some interest," but ultimately declined and suggested the dealer propose it to William Randolph Hearst, whose collecting will be discussed in greater detail below. Kagan, *Spanish Craze*, 269–71. In 1941 Blumenthal bequeathed the patio to the Metropolitan Museum of Art, where it has been reassembled.

10. Marcus B. Burke, "Archer Milton Huntington and the Hispanic Society of America," in Colomer and Reist, *Collecting Spanish Art*, 203.

11. Victoria Rodríguez Thiessen, "Byne and Stapley: Scholars, Dealers, and Collectors of Spanish Decorative Arts" (MA thesis, Cooper-Hewitt Museum and Parsons School of Design, 1998), 6, citing Byne to Huntington, December 13, 1913, Huntington Correspondence, Hispanic Society Museum & Library Archives (hereafter cited as HSA)

12. *A History of the Hispanic Society of America Museum and Library: 1904–1954* (Hispanic Society of America, 1954), 45.

13. *Rejería of the Spanish Renaissance* (De Vinne, 1914); *Spanish Ironwork* (Hispanic Society of America, 1915); *Spanish Architecture of the Sixteenth Century* (G.P. Putnam's Sons, 1917); *Decorated Wooden Ceilings in Spain* (G.P. Putnam's Sons, 1920); *Spanish Interiors and Furniture*, 3 vols. (W. Helburn, 1921–25); *Spanish Gardens and Patios* (J.B. Lippincott and Architectural Record, 1924); *Provincial Houses in Spain* (W. Helburn, 1925); and *Majorcan Houses and Gardens: A Spanish Island in the Mediterranean* (W. Helburn, 1928). Stapley was the sole author of *Christopher Columbus* (Macmillan, 1915); *Popular Weaving and Embroidery in Spain* (W. Helburn, 1924); *The Sculptured Capital in Spain* (W. Helburn, 1926); and *Forgotten Shrines of Spain* (J.B. Lippincott, 1926).

14. Byne and Stapley, *Spanish Architecture*, iii.

15. Byne to Huntington, October 25, 1919, Huntington's Correspondence, HSA, cited in Rodríguez Thiessen, "Byne and Stapley," 15.

16. Rodríguez Thiessen, *Byne and Stapley*, 26, citing Dionisio Pérez, "Enamorados del arte español: Una obra admirable de hispanización," ABC (Madrid), July 9, 1922, 2; translated in "New Haven Man Is International Authority on Spanish Art," *New Haven Register*, September 17, 1922, 3.

17. Arthur Colton, "The Architect's Library," *Architectural Record* 57 (June 1925): 579.

18. Mitchell Codding, "Archer Milton Huntington, Champion of Spain in the United States," in *Spain in America: The Origins of Hispanism in the United States*, ed. Richard L. Kagan (University of Illinois Press, 2002), 161.

19. Rodríguez Thiessen, "Byne and Stapley," 8, 14–15, citing Huntington's notes, January 4, 1919, Huntington's Correspondence, HSA.

20. Victoria Kastner, *Julia Morgan: An Intimate Biography of the Trailblazing Architect* (Chronicle, 2021); and Sara Holmes Boutelle, *Julia Morgan, Architect* (Abbeville, 1995).

21. Stapley to Morgan, April 28, 1914, Julia Morgan Papers, Special Collections and Archives, California Polytechnic State University, San Luis Obispo, MS 010 (hereafter cited as JMP), box 44, folder 1, 1914. Three letters from Stapley to Morgan regarding this possible sale are preserved, with the other two dating to June 9 and 19. Stapley specifies that the photographs must be purchased for personal use and not publication, as the Hispanic Society held their copyright and notes that copies of the photographs had already been purchased by the Hispanic Society, the Metropolitan Museum of Art, Harvard University, the Massachusetts Institute of Technology, and Avery Library at Columbia University.

22. José Miguel Merino de Cáceres and María José Martínez Ruiz, *La destrucción del patrimonio artístico español: W.R. Hearst, 'el gran acaparador'* (Cátedra, 2012); and Mary L. Levkoff, *Hearst the Collector*, exh. cat. (Harry N. Abrams and Los Angeles County Museum of Art, 2008). More recently the historian Richard Kagan has argued that Hearst's staunchly pro-American and pro-democracy views, combined with his contempt for European monarchies, were at the heart of his collecting preferences. Kagan, *Spanish Craze*, 284–88.

23. Morgan to Stapley, September 19, 1921, JMP, box 44, folder 2.

24. Levkoff (*Hearst the Collector*, 57) suggests that he may have interpreted this architecture as a mixture of a Swiss chalet and Japanese shrines.

25. Stapley to Morgan, October 1, 1921, JMP, box 44, folder 2.

26. Morgan to Byne and Stapley, November 1, 1921, JMP, box 44, folder 2.

27. Morgan to Byne and Stapley, November 18, 1921, quoting from a cablegram from Hearst, JMP, box 44, folder 2.

28. Byne to Morgan, December 15, 1921, JMP, box 44, folder 2.

29. Kagan, *Spanish Craze*, 14, 287.

30. Mary L. Levkoff, "Hearst and Spain," in Colomer and Reist, *Collecting Spanish Art*, 188.

31. Levkoff, "Hearst and Spain," 181–82.

32. Morgan to Hearst, January 5, 1920, JMP, box 47, folder 6: "Last summer I started to tell you of the wonderful collection of Spanish photographs made by Mr. and Mrs. Byne whose book 'Spanish Architecture of the 16th Century' you sent me."

33. Byne to Morgan, June 5, 1924, JMP, box 44, folder 5. Joseph Duveen (1869–1939) and Jacques Seligmann (1858–1923) were among the most influential art dealers of the early twentieth century, each helming major firms (Duveen Brothers and Jacques Seligmann & Company) with prominent clients across Europe and the United States.

34. David Nasaw, *The Chief: The Life of William Randolph Hearst* (Houghton Mifflin, 2000), 301. Located on 143rd Street near Southern Boulevard, the International Studio Art Corporation employed approximately twenty people.

35. Byne to Morgan, September 14, 1925, JMP, box 44, folder 14; and Levkoff, "Hearst and Spain," 197.

36. Sarah Slingluff, "Protecting Spanish Cultural Heritage at the Beginning of the 20th Century," *V&A Blog*, Victoria & Albert Museum, April 23, 2025, https://www.vam.ac.uk/blog/projects/protecting-spanish-cultural-heritage-at-the-beginning-of-the-20th-century.

37. Levkoff, *Hearst the Collector*, 63–64.

38. For a summary of these developments, see Kagan, *Spanish Craze*, 299–302; Merino de Cáceres and Martínez Ruiz, *La destrucción del patrimonio*, 23–48; and Slinghuff, "Protecting Spanish Cultural Heritage."

39. Mozzati, "Vélez Blanco Patio," 53.

40. For a fuller account of this episode, see Kagan, *Spanish Craze*, 288–90; and María José Martínez Ruiz, "La Casa Miranda de Burgos: La defensa ante la posible salida al extranjero de su patio," *Boletín del Seminario de Estudios de Arte y Arqueología* 66 (2000): 181–98.

41. Throughout this text, calculations of 2024 USD amounts have been made using the Bureau of Labor Statistics CPI Inflation Calculator: https://data.bls.gov/cgi-bin/cpicalc.pl.

42. "The Pride of Burgos," *New York Times*, November 3, 1910.

43. Hearst to Morgan, December 19, 1919, JMP, box 47, folder 5.

44. Byne to Morgan, July 4, 1925, JMP, box 44, folder 12: "Contemplating the sale of this cloister and Chapter House one recalls the sum paid by the Metropolitan Museum a few months ago for the cloister of George Barnard—if I am not mistaken it was $600,000."

45. Byne to Morgan, September 25, 1925, JMP, box 44, folder 14.

46. The decree was published in the *Gaceta de Madrid* on June 4, 1931. In addition to proposing 755 new national artistic treasures, it declared that several properties belonging to the Spanish crown would receive official protection. See Slingluff, "Protecting Spanish Cultural Heritage."

47. Byne to Hearst, July 19, 1931, JMP, box 45, folder 26.

48. Levkoff, "Hearst and Spain," 197n44, citing Hearst to Joseph Willicombe (Hearst's secretary), written in Seville, Spain, summer 1934; auctioned at "William Randolph Hearst: The Collection of John F. Dunlap" (sale 282), PBA Galleries, San Francisco, March 25, 2004, lot 15.

49. The first reference to this appears in a telegram from Morgan to Byne on July 23, 1925: "FIND US ANOTHER CLOISTER." JMP, box 44, folder 12. My understanding of the following episode is indebted to the scholarship in José Miguel Merino de Cáceres and María José Martínez Ruiz, "Arthur Byne, Mildred Stapley, José Costa y el patio de la Casa Ayamans (Palma de Mallorca): Detalles de un despojo artístico en el contexto de la promoción turística balear," *Espacio, tiempo y forma* 7, no. 10 (2022): 121–50.

50. Morgan to Byne, August 18, 1925, JMP, box 44, folder 13.

51. Morgan to Byne, August 25, 1925, JMP, box 44, folder 13. Byne responded that he "never received any such list; it would help me very much to have a list of what strikes Mr. Hearst's fancy." He asked Morgan to send another copy. Byne to Morgan, September 25, 1925, JMP, box 44, folder 14.

52. Hearst to Morgan, December 9, 1925, JMP, box 44, folder 17.

53. Morgan to Byne, March 5, 1926, JMP, box 45, folder 3. As the Casa Grande at San Simeon neared completion (it was dedicated in 1926), Hearst made plans for a beach house for his companion, Marion Davies, in Santa Monica. The ultimate structure was a Georgian-style mansion, which surely would not have accommodated this patio.

54. Byne to Morgan, March 25, 1929, JMP, box 45, folder 14.

55. Morgan would sometimes make copies of photographs Byne sent for her files or ask him to send duplicates, explaining: "It is always hopeless to get a photograph back from Mr. Hearst.... They keep no files for Mr. Hearst personally, and as he moves about much, I suppose his secretaries become desparate [*sic*]." Morgan to Byne, December 24, 1929, JMP, box 55, folder 6.

56. Byne to Morgan, April 14, 1929, JMP, box 45, folder 14.

57. On the construction of the hotel, see Francisca Lladó Pol, "Mecenazgo argentino en Mallorca: Adán Diehl, Carlos Tornquist y el Hotel Formentor," *Revista de instituciones, ideas y mercados*, no. 59 (October 2013): 79–100.

58. Morgan to Byne, April 15, 1929, JMP, box 45, folder 14.

59. Pablo Piferrer and José María Quadrado, *Islas Baleares*, vol. 27 of *España: Sus monumentos y artes, su naturaleza e historia* (Barcelona, 1888), 654.

60. Byne to Morgan, July 14, 1929, JMP, box 45, folder 14.

61. Byne to Hearst, September 12, 1929, JMP, box 45, folder 14.

62. Byne to Morgan, November 1, 1929, JMP, box 45, folder 14: "Yesterday I mailed to you a number of prints of rectified drawings of the Palma patio, the Gothic stair."

63. It is possible that between March and July, Byne changed the stairway included in the ensemble. Merino de Cáceres and Martínez Ruiz, "Arthur Byne," 140, cite a May 10, 1929, letter from Byne to Costa in which Byne notes that he needs to prepare drawings of the ensemble and wants to see if it is possible to combine the stones from another staircase Sacanell is restoring with those from the Ayamans patio. The authors suggest that Byne purchased the stones from Can Oleo.

64. The 160 albums of Hearst's Bronx inventory are stored at the William Randolph Hearst Archive, Long Island University. The Princeton patio was registered in album 83, item no. 6, pp. 19–22 (lot 275, nos. 1–65).

65. The sheets in Princeton's files are numbered 19 to 22, which corresponds to the page numbering system of the International Studio Art Corporation album.

66. Byne to Morgan, April 27, 1929, JMP, box 45, folder 14.

67. Their photographic expedition funded by the Hispanic Society dates to 1915. By 1922 they were spending significant periods of time on the island; in a letter to Morgan, Stapley writes: "Put Mallorca on your list as a place that must be seen. We have taken a casita for three months.... Venerable masonry, venerable olive orchards, simple friendly people who probably have not altered in speech or customs since the middle ages. Plan for a sabbatical year and come." Stapley to Morgan, January 2, 1922, JMP, box 44, folder 3.

68. Byne and Stapley, *Majorcan Houses and Gardens*, front matter.

69. Stapley to Helen Strong, January 7, 1928, SWG, part 1, box 6, folder 3.

70. Eduard Moyà, *Journeys in the Sun: Travel Literature and Desire in the Balearic Islands (1903–1939)* (Peter Lang, 2017); and Eduard Moyà, "American Travelers in Mallorca in the Twentieth Century: The Hard Work of the Nothing-to-Do's," *Revista de filología* 38 (January 2019): 169–83.

71. Merino de Cáceres and Martínez Ruiz, "Arthur Byne," 125–26.

72. Merino de Cáceres and Martínez Ruiz, "Arthur Byne," 125–26.

73. Maria Josep Mulet Gutiérrez, "Fotògrafs de projecció internacional a les Balears: Motivacions i objectius," *Estudis baleàrics*, no. 94–95 (2008–9): 100; and Alberto Velasco González, "Josep Costa Ferrer (1876–1971), antiquari i agent del mercat de l'art entre Barcelona i Palma," in *Mercat de l'art, col·leccionisme i museus*, ed. Bonaventura Bassegoda and Ignasi Domènech (Universitat Autònoma de Barcelona, 2023), 209.

74. These details are based on Costa's recollection several years later, as published by Luis Ripoll, "Notas sobre unas piedras viejas y su traslado a Norteamérica," *Papeles de Son Armadans*, no. 89 (August 1963): 265–71.

75. These calculations were made using an exchange rate of approximately 7 pesetas to 1 USD in both 1925 and 1929 and were based on Banco de España, "Tipos de cambio de la peseta frente al franco francés, la libra esterlina y el dólar estadounidense (1880–1998), version 1 [dataset]," 2021, Repositorio institucional del Banco de España, https://repositorio.bde.es/handle/123456789/15657.

76. Merino de Cáceres and Martínez Ruiz, "Arthur Byne," 137, citing the personal archives of Josep Costa Ferrer. It is striking that Costa was often praised for his contributions to the preservation of Mallorcan art and architecture while he was also an active player in the international art market. See, for example, Gabriel Alomar, "Nuevas ordenanzas municipales

para la zona historico-monumental de Palma de Mallorca," *Revista Nacional de Arquitectura* 3, no. 31 (July 1944): 257–62, in which the author contrasts Byne's purchase of the Ayamans patio (259) with Costa's preservation of a historic window (262), without acknowledging Costa's role in the Ayamans sale.

77. "Inventory: Estate of the Late Mrs. Stapley Byne," 1942, National Archives and Records Administration, Civil Records Branch. Reproduced in Rodríguez Thiessen, "Byne and Stapley," appendix.

78. *French Furniture ... Property of Various Owners Including the Estate of the Late Mildred Stapley Byne*, sale cat. (Parke-Bernet Galleries, June 4–5, 1942).

79. Merino de Cáceres and Martínez Ruiz, "Arthur Byne," 144–45.

80. Merino de Cáceres and Martínez Ruiz, "Arthur Byne," 143, citing "Baleares," *El Sol*, January 17, 1929, 4: "tanto indígenas como extranjeros."

81. Board of trustees of the Hispanic Society to Mildred Stapley Byne, November 2, 1935, HSA, Mildred Stapley Byne, Members File.

82. Ruiz Mas, "Early Twentieth-Century American Travelers"; Merino de Cáceres and Martínez Ruiz, "Arthur Byne"; and Immaculada Socias Batet and Dimitra Gkozgkou, *Agentes, marchantes y traficantes de objetos de arte (1850–1950)* (Trea, 2012), 108.

83. María José Martínez Ruiz, "Mildred Stapley: 'Esta mujer trabajadora, que tiene un expert conocimiento de la arquitectura española, ¿es acaso una feminista inaguantable?,'" in *Ellas siempre han estado ahí: Coleccionismo y mujeres*, ed. Patricia Andrés González and Miguel Ángel Zalama (Doce Calles, 2019), 201, citing L.T.B., "Majorcan Houses and Gardens," *Arquitectura* 115 (1928): "Nunca les agradeceremos bastante su labor de propaganda y vulgarización, sobre todo, aunque haya traído inevitablemente consigo la dolorsa emigración de no pocas de nuestras obras del arte antiguo a los museos y colecciones de Norteamérica. Los Sres. Byne han contribuido también en no corta medida al desarrollo de los estudios de arte hispánico en su país de origen" (27).

84. "Arthur Byne Dies in Spain," *New York Times*, July 17, 1935.

85. A recent and nuanced intervention on this topic is offered by José María Sadia, *El autoexpolio del patrimonio español: Cuando España malvendió su arte* (Almuzara, 2022), who introduces a new term for the role that Spaniards played in dismantling architecture and allowing it to be exported to international collectors: *autoexpolio*, or "self-plunder." I am grateful to Cristina Aldrich for sharing this reference with me.

86. American museums also made this argument. Around the same time, the director of the Met, James Rorimer, wrote of a Catalan tomb monument acquired by the museum: "This monument, tomb of Armengol VII, Count of Urgel, had been frequently described in local publications previous to 1906, at which time almost all of the sculptures were definitely removed from the monastery. It was erroneously stated at the time, with characteristic Spanish indignation in such matters, that the important tombs from the monastery had been sent to England and were to be installed in a museum there. For almost twenty-five years the finest of the finest of the tombs, that of Armengol VII, the founder of the monastery, had been forgotten by all but a few 'antiquaries,' who had saved the monument from what might have been its complete ruination had it been left in Spain, and have seen it transferred to the care of the Metropolitan Museum of Art." James J. Rorimer, "A Fourteenth Century Catalan Tomb at the Cloisters and Related Monuments," *Art Bulletin* 13, no. 4 (December 1931): 409. I am grateful to Cristina Aldrich for sharing this reference with me.

87. Mildred Stapley, "Literature and Sworn Testimony," *Architectural Record* 47 (1924): 383.

88. Levkoff, *Hearst the Collector*, 63.

89. The stairway and patio do not appear in the San Simeon Warehouse Inventory. I am grateful to Cara O'Brien, museum director, Hearst San Simeon State Historical Monument, for consulting the San Simeon inventory.

90. Morgan to Byne, April 7, 1930, JMP, box 45, folder 18. Around August 1926 Hearst and Morgan began discussing Hearst's intention to build two additional guesthouses for San Simeon, houses D and E, which he wanted to make "rather more luxurious" than the existing guesthouses A, B, and C. Neither house was built. See Kastner, *Julia Morgan*, 226n35. I am grateful to Carrie Arnold, guide II supervisor, Hearst San Simeon State Historical Monument, for alerting me to this reference.

91. JMP, box 45, folder 26: "CEILINGS *NOT* IN CALIFORNIA."

92. Nasaw, *The Chief*, 488–99.

93. Shearn divided the value of the collection in half, allocating $11.5 million of art and antiques to Hearst and $11.5 million to the International Studio Art Corporation; Hearst was able to alter the contents of the lists, provided he substituted items of equal value. Nasaw, *The Chief*, 540.

94. Nasaw, *The Chief*, 529–42, 554–56; and Levkoff, *Hearst the Collector*, 125–32.

95. "Hearst Collection of Art to Be Sold by 2 Stores Here," *New York Times*, December 29, 1940.

96. "Commodities: Major Liquidation," *Time*, January 6, 1941, https://time.com/archive/6764532/commodities-major-liquidation/; and "Hearst Collection of Art."

97. "Publisher Spent Millions for Art," *New York Times*, August 15, 1951.

98. "Hearst Sale Held a Lesson to Spain: Never Again Would She Let Such Treasures Go, Falange Paper Says of Monastery," *New York Times*, January 4, 1941.

99. *Art Objects & Furnishings from the William Randolph Hearst Collection: Catalogue Raisonné Comprising Illustrations of Representative Works Together with Comprehensive Descriptions of Books, Autographs and Manuscripts and Complete Index* (Hammer Galleries, 1941), 322, lot 275, nos. 1–65. The Ayamans ceilings were sold at Gimbel Brothers as well: lot 351, nos. 1–17, as coming "from the Alemany Palace." The inclusion of "catalogue raisonné" in the title is misleading; the publication is a perfunctory list.

100. "List or Manifest of Alien Passengers for the United States Immigrant Inspector at Port of Arrival: S.S. Excambion, Passengers Sailing from Lisbon, Portugal, November 19, 1940," National Archives, Passenger and Crew Lists of Vessels Arriving at New York, New York, 1897–1957, Record Group 85: Records of the Immigration and Naturalization Service. Pick's name is given on the manifest as Zelie Emilienne Marguerite Pick, although she later went simply by Marguerite. An additional companion listed is Francine Berthel van Landuyt, whose occupation is given as "student."

101. Jean Germain Léon Cassel denied Nazi claims that he was Jewish and had obtained parentage papers to prove his Aryanism, but his grandmother was Julie Stern, a member of the Jewish banking family from Frankfurt. In a speech given during a March 11, 2014, restitution ceremony held by the Ministère de la Culture in France, the baron's granddaughter, Jacqueline Domeyko, described the Cassel family as being of "Jewish origin." The ceremony is accessible online: https://www.dailymotion.com/video/x1gdekr. The Cassel family is included in Jacques Déom et al., *Les juifs en Belgique: Guide bibliographique* (Fondation de la Mémoire Contemporaine, 2014).

102. "Cassel," in *Biographie nationale* (L'Académie Royale des Sciences, des Lettres et des Beaux-Arts de Belgique, 1977), 40:112–21.

103. "Baron Leon Cassel, Belgian Banker, Dies," *Boston Globe*, January 13, 1930: "[He] was known as an art lover and the owner of a valuable picture gallery" (15).

104. "Baron's Evening Wedding," *Daily Telegraph*, December 14, 1934, 17.

105. The baron wrote in 1946: "The explanation of the apparent discrepancy between the name Cassel and Cassel van Doorn is that, a few years ago, for family reasons, we decided to join my wife's family name to mine which, is quite customary in Belgium." Baron Cassel to S. Lane Faison, March 7, 1946, National Archives, Record Group 260: Records of U.S. Occupation Headquarters, World War II: Restitution Claim Records (NAID 34727537); Restitution Cases: General Correspondence—France Claims, January 1946–April 1946.

106. Jean Louis A. de Riquelès, former lawyer at court of Paris, secretary general of Banque Cassel in Brussels to M. [Paulin] Colonna d'Istria, judge in military tribunal of Nice, October 19, 1944, National Archives, Record Group 260: Records of U.S. Occupation Headquarters, World War II: Cultural Property Claim Applications: F31B Cassel, Jean Baron Van Doorn "Bertha Cassel" France (NAID 91220525).

107. Baron Cassel van Doorn to Lt. Craig Smyth, head of Central Collecting Point in Munich, March 8, 1946, National Archives, Record Group 260: Records of U.S. Occupation Headquarters, World War II: Restitution Claim Records: Restitution Cases: General Correspondence—France Claims, January 1946–April 1946 (NAID 34727537).

108. Cassel van Doorn to Smyth, March 8, 1946.

109. This is suggested in a letter written by S. Lane Faison after speaking to Cassel: "He certified all US banks with whom he had (considerable) accounts that they were not to answer inquiries as to his holdings. One bank, which he describes as the 'largest in the US,' failed to comply. He says the manager of the Foreign Dept of this bank was and still is potentially a Nazi agent. He has repeated this in person to FBI (Nichols, in absence of Hoover). *Charles Gray (Paris)*, he says know the story." Faison to Otto Wittmann, March 1, 1946, National Archives, Record Group 239: Records of the American Commission for the Protection and

Salvage of Artistic and Historic Monuments in War Areas, Subject Files: Confiscated Collections, 1940–1946 (NAID 66884822).

110. "Dutch Nobility Here," *Press of Atlantic City*, October 13, 1941, 1; and "Bergen Rent Suit Decision Reserved [*sic*]," *Herald News* (Passaic, NJ), October 16, 1943, 11.

111. "Statement of the Case," *Jean G.L. and Marij V. Cassel van Doorn v. William Henig*, Supreme Court of the United States, October term, 1951, no. 613, 34.

112. According to news reports after his death, the baron had a romance with a young woman who came to live there between 1926 and 1929; after her death in 1929, he closed the manor, although it remained completely furnished and he maintained a gardener. The contents of the manor were auctioned after his death, by order of the executors of his estate. See "Mystery of the Manor," *Chronicle* (Adelaide, Australia), September 30, 1954, 53; and "Baron's Manor, Locked-Up for 25 Years, Yields It's [*sic*] Secrets," *Evening Standard* (London), April 30, 1955, 3.

113. "Queen Wilhelmina Not Moving to Englewood," *Herald News* (Passaic, NJ), September 26, 1944, 18.

114. Faison to Wittmann, March 1, 1946.

115. "Brief of Respondent in Opposition," *Jean G.L. and Marij V. Cassel van Doorn*, 4.

116. The table now in the Metropolitan Museum of Art is Bernard II van Risenburgh, Writing table (table à écrire), ca. 1755 (1976.155.100). It was sold at Parke-Bernet Galleries, New York, May 3, 1941, lot 1420. In an entry on a related piece now in the Getty Museum, the authors cite J. Paul Getty's annotated copy of the Parke-Bernet sale. Gillian Wilson, Arlen Heginbotham, and Yannick Chastang, "Writing Table," in *French Rococo Ébénisterie in the J. Paul Getty Museum*, ed. Gillian Wilson and Arlen Heginbotham (J. Paul Getty Museum, 2021), no. 9, https://www.getty.edu/publications/rococo/catalogue/9/. At the same sale, the baron also likely purchased for $4,700 an eighteenth-century secretaire by René Dubois now in the Getty Museum (72.DA.60).

117. Barnard's "Abbaye," as it was called, was partially acquired by the Philadelphia Museum of Art and partially sold by Plaza Art Galleries, New York (December 13, 1945, lot 56), where the baron purchased it. It later entered the collection of the Carnegie Museum of Art, Pittsburgh. It was deaccessioned and sold at Christie's, New York, on October 7, 2008 (live auction no. 2105, lot 48).

118. John Edgar Hoover to the director, Strategic Service Unit, War Department, March 15, 1946, National Archives, Record Group 239: Records of the American Commission for the Protection and Salvage of Artistic and Historic Monuments in War Areas, Subject Files: Confiscated Collections, 1940–1946 (NAID 66884822).

119. "Note pour Mr. de Ricqlès à propos du vol commis par les Allemands à Ruoms, en fin Décembre 1943 au préjudice de M. CASSEL et S.O.F.I.M.I," National Archives, Record Group 260: Records of U.S. Occupation Headquarters, World War II, Selected Records: From: folder 182, Claims–Belgium to: folder 185, Claims–Belgium (NAID 175154127): "Celui qui dirigeait a dit que M. Cassel était Juif 100%. J'ai voulu montrer copie de papiers de filiation prouvant qu'au regard de la loi française M. Cassel ne pouvait être considéré comme juif, ainsi que copie de l'arrêté relevant le commissaire de ses fonctions. Il m'a été répondu que ces papiers ne les intéressaient pas, que M. Cassel avait été naturalisé Juif américain, qu'il était en dissidence et qu'ils avaient vu, à propos de cette naturalisation, une note sur le bureau de M. Darquier de Pellequoi. En arrivant, ils connaissaient déjà mon nom, savaient que j'avais chez moi des biens de M. Cassel.... Il a prétendu être porteur d'un mandat d'arrêt contre moi mais ne me l'a pas montré.... Je n'ai pu sauver qu'un carton où j'avais réuni ce qui me paraissait le mieux comme dessins et gravures, entre leurs deux visites et que j'avais dissimulé dans une penderie de vêtements. En partant, ils réclamèrent les certificats de filiation que j'avais voulu leur montrer et les emportèrent. Des camions (de dix à douze) ... sont venus faire le déménagement. Ils étaient accompagnés d'une trentaine d'Allemands."

120. Julian Jackson, *France: The Dark Years, 1940–1944* (Oxford University Press, 2001), 230–32.

121. Cassel van Doorn to Smyth, March 8, 1946.

122. S.L. Faison, "Consolidated Interrogation Report No. 4, December 15, 1945: Linz: Hitler's Museum and Library" (NAID 148374229), chap. 5, 61, National Archives, Record Group 239: Records of the American Commission for the Protection and Salvage of Artistic and Historic Monuments in War Areas, Consolidated Interrogation Reports. Calculation of 2024 value is based on a historical conversion with the 1940 rate of 1 USD = 2.50 reichsmark.

123. National Archives, Record Group 260: Records of U.S.

Occupation Headquarters, World War II, General Administrative Records: Alt-Ausee Salt Mine, File No. R&R #2 (NAID: 93236982).
124. Faison to Wittmann, March 1, 1946.
125. The Database of Art Objects at the Jeu de Paume (Einsatzstab Reichsleiter Rosenberg [ERR] database) associates 4,328 objects with the Cassel van Doorns, including functional objects such as kitchen utensils. The number 3,478 was given by the family in a March 11, 2014, restitution ceremony held by the Ministère de la Culture in France. Laurent Carpentier, "Trois tableaux volés par les nazis restitués par la France," *Le Monde*, March 11, 2014.
126. Doreen Carvajal, "France Returns Three Paintings Looted by Nazis," *New York Times*, March 11, 2014.
127. "$40,000 Art Treaures Here Released to Belgian Owner," *Edmonton Journal*, October 21, 1950, p. 19.
128. "Bergen Legacy Tops $600,000," *Record* (Hackensack, NJ), November 23, 1956, 4.
129. In addition to sales of smaller groups of objects held throughout the 1950s, the sales of the Cassel van Doorn estate included *The Art Reference Library of the Estate of the Late Baron Cassel van Doorn*, Parke-Bernet Galleries, New York, January 12–13, 1954; *Tableaux anciens, estampes, objets d'art et de bel ameublement … tapisseries du XVe au XIIIe siècle provenant des collections réunies par le Baron Cassel et la Baronesse Cassel van Doorn*, Galerie Charpentier, Paris, March 9, 1954; and *Notable French Eighteenth Century Furniture & Objets d'Art … Property of the Estate of the Late Baron Cassel van Doorn*, Parke-Bernet Galleries, New York, December 9 and 10, 1955. The baroness held an additional sale of her collection: *Collection de la Baronne Cassel Van Doorn: Tableaux anciens … objets d'art et de bel ameublement du XVIIIe siècle, tapisseries gothiques et du XVIIIe siècle, tapis, …* Paris, Galerie Charpentier, May 30, 1956.
130. Ernest T. DeWald to Arthur E. Fox, October 16, 1955, Princeton University, Office of the President Records: Robert F. Goheen (AC #193), box 515, folder 13, series 18.2, Van Doorn, Baroness Cassel, 1955.
131. Carl Otto Kienbusch to Patrick J. Kelleher, August 19, 1963, Baroness Cassel van Doorn Donor File, Princeton University Art Museum.
132. The three doorways are y1955-3283, y1955-3284, y1955-3287. The two sculptures are y1955-3260 and y1955-3273, and the window is y1955-3285.
133. DeWald to Fox, October 16, 1955.
134. "Mansion, Estate Bought by Jewish Congregation," *Record* (Hackensack, NJ), August 20, 1958, 4.
135. Marguerite Pick to Patrick J. Kelleher, June 10, 1965, and Patrick J. Kelleher to Mrs. Alexander, c/o Marguerite Pick, June 30, 1965, Baroness Cassel van Doorn Donor File.

Elena Torok
pages 89–137

1. Not all of these elements were included in the 2025 installation.
2. Four of the five newel posts included with the elements today were fabricated in the United States. The fifth newel post was fabricated in Mallorca, but its source is not known. (See the section "Arrival at Princeton and Installation in the Former Museum Building, 1955–66" below.) As Alexandra Letvin mentions in the introduction to this volume, Can Ayamans has also historically been referred to as Posada de s'Estorell or Can Pacs-Fuster.
3. I am indebted to the scholarship of José Miguel Merino de Cáceres and María José Martínez Ruiz, whose research was foundational in understanding the ensemble's origins and formation. José Miguel Merino de Cáceres and María José Martínez Ruiz, "Arthur Byne, Mildred Stapley, José Costa y el patio de la Casa Ayamans (Palma de Mallorca): Detalles de un despojo artístico en el contexto de la promoción turística balear," *Espacio, tiempo y forma* 7, no. 10 (2022): 121–50.
4. Costa's account of acquiring and restoring the elements from Can Ayamans (as well as his inability to find a local buyer) was published by Luis Ripoll, "Notas sobre unas piedras viejas y su traslado a Norteamérica," *Papeles de Son Armadans*, no. 89 (August 1963): 265–71. Additional information on his work with Byne to prepare the group of elements for sale can be found in the private archive of Elena Costa Gispert (hereafter cited as Costa Archive), as published by Merino de Cáceres and Martínez Ruiz, "Arthur Byne," 137–40.
5. Byne's acquisition of a stairway from Costa was outlined in Merino de Cáceres and Martínez Ruiz, "Arthur Byne," 140. The authors cite correspondence from the Costa Archive. Byne's sale to Hearst was confirmed in Julia Morgan to Arthur Byne, April 15, 1929, Julia Morgan Papers, Special Collections and Archives, California Polytechnic State University, San Luis Obispo,

MS 010 (hereafter cited as JMP), box 45, folder 14.

6. *Art Objects & Furnishings from the William Randolph Hearst Collection: Catalogue Raisonné Comprising Illustrations of Representative Works Together with Comprehensive Descriptions of Books, Autographs and Manuscripts and Complete Index*, sale cat. (Hammer Galleries, 1941), 322, lot 275, nos. 1–65.

7. For an account of Baron Cassel van Doorn's acquisition of this architectural composition, see Letvin, this volume. Information on the gift to Princeton University is in Carl Otto Kienbusch to Patrick J. Kelleher, August 19, 1963, Baroness Cassel van Doorn Donor File, Princeton University Art Museum.

8. Kelly Caldwell, EverGreene Architectural Arts, "Princeton University Art Museum Spanish Stairs Treatment Report," February 8, 2024, Conservation File, Princeton University Art Museum; and additional discussion with Kelly Caldwell.

9. Sacanell is identified by Costa in Ripoll, "Notas sobre unas piedras viejas," 271 (though referenced there as José). Sacanell's involvement in the restoration of the Claustro de San Francisco is mentioned in María Pilar García Cuetos, "La recuperación del claustro del Convento de San Francisco de Palma de Jeroni Martorell a Alejandro Ferrant: Restauración científica frente unidad visual," *Norba: Revista de arte*, no. 42 (2022): 103.

10. Ripoll, "Notas sobre unas piedras viejas," 271. Arthur Byne to Josep Costa, May 10, 1929, Costa Archive, as cited by Merino de Cáceres and Martínez Ruiz, "Arthur Byne," 140.

11. This floor plan was rendered by Merino de Cáceres in Merino de Cáceres and Martínez Ruiz, "Arthur Byne," 135, fig. 6.

12. Photograph labeled "Casa Ayamans," digitized from the album "Família Ciaudo: Una estada a Mallorca al 1895," 1895, Cabot Umbert Collection, Arxiu del So i de la Imatge de Mallorca, Palma de Mallorca, Spain, https://www.flickr.com/photos/arxiudelsoidelaimatgemallorca/51874003077/in/album-72177720296608601.

13. Fotos Antiguas de Mallorca—FAM, "José María Marco nos remite una nueva fotografía, del álbum que le lego su abuelo. Se trata de un típico patio mallorquín, el cual no reconocíamos, pero gracias a nuestro amigo e historiador Roberto Fernández Legido que lo ha reconocido y nos envía la siguiente información: 'Aquesta foto és irrepetible perquè es tracta del pati de Can Pacs-Fuster, del qual actualment només en resten les columnes i l'arc de pas. La resta fou traslladat als Estats Units el 1929. Va ser un dels espolis que patí el patrimoni de la ciutat en aquella època.'" Facebook, June 28, 2013, https://www.facebook.com/fotosantiguasdemallorca/photos/a.468574586518607/569579283084803.

14. Archduke Ludwig Salvator of Austria, *Die Balearen in Wort und Bild geschildert*, vol. 1 (Leipzig, 1897), 403, plate 51*; Pablo Piferrer and José María Quadrado, *Islas Baleares*, vol. 27 of *España: Sus monumentos y artes, su naturaleza e historia* (Barcelona, 1888), 653; and Álvaro Campaner y Fuertes, *Cronicón Mayoricense: Noticias y relaciones históricas de Mallorca desde 1229 a 1800* (Palma de Mallorca, 1881), plate VII.

15. The interior of the first patio is visible today from the front entrance of the residence on Carrer d'en Morei.

16. For more information about the surviving door lintel with inscription, see Piferrer and Quadrado, *Islas Baleares*, 654; Magdalena de Quiroga Conrado, "La emblemática caballeresca en la Mallorca del renacimiento (siglos XV–XVI): Las cimeras y las divisas," *Memòries de la Reial Acadèmia Mallorquina d'Estudis Genealògics, Heràldics i Històrics*, no. 19 (2009): 50–51; and Gabriel Alomar Esteve, "Antiguas inscripciones lapidarias en las calles y patios de la ciudad de Palma," *Papeles de Son Armadans* 17, no. 50 (1960): 191.

17. Quiroga Conrado, "La emblemática caballeresca," 50.

18. Museu de Mallorca, Palma, inv. no. DA05/14/0056.

19. A skim coat is a thin layer of material (typically plaster or cement) applied to a stone's surface to smooth or unify its overall appearance.

20. These elements are not included in the current display.

21. These elements are not included in the current display.

22. Josep Costa, handwritten note, June 1, 1929, Costa Archive, as cited by Merino de Cáceres and Martínez Ruiz, "Arthur Byne," 140. The authors' summary of this note is in Spanish: "cinco columnas enteras labradas; tres cajas con 'basas de columna grabadas'; nueve cajas con piezas de 'Barandilla galería gótica'; dos columnas partidas labradas y cuatro medias columnas a pared labradas; una base columna labrada y dos medias 'base o zócalo columna labrada'; tres capiteles de columnas; siete basas; marcos de ventana y cuatro capiteles; otras dos medias columnas en trozos y un número considerable de trozos de moldura y zócalo." I am grateful to Cristina Aldrich for her help with English translation.

23. Byne to Costa, May 10, 1929, Costa Archive, as cited by Merino de Cáceres and Martínez Ruiz, "Arthur Byne," 140.
24. The overall weight of the 1929 shipment was recorded by Costa, handwritten note, June 1, 1929, Costa Archive, as cited by Merino de Cáceres and Martínez Ruiz, "Arthur Byne," 140. In 2021 the total weight of all elements (without crates) was estimated by EverGreene Architectural Arts to be more than 21,000 pounds, and the combined weight of columns, balustrades, and three nonoriginal newel posts (without crates) was estimated by EverGreene Architectural Arts to be between 13,000 and 14,000 pounds.
25. For additional information on now-missing elements, see the sections "Early Years in the United States, 1929–55" and "Arrival at Princeton and Installation in the Former Museum Building, 1955–66" below.
26. Arthur Byne and Mildred Stapley Byne, *Majorcan Houses and Gardens: A Spanish Island in the Mediterranean* (W. Helburn, 1928), plate 160. In recent years this drawing has been connected to the Can Ayamans elements sold in 1929 by Arthur Byne to William Randolph Hearst: see Miquel À. Capellà Galmés and Joan Domenge i Mesquida, "La escalera en los patios señoriales de Palma de Mallorca: Tipología y ornamentación," *LEXICON: Storie e architettura in Sicilia*, special issue no. 2 (2021): 401; and Merino de Cáceres and Martínez Ruiz, "Arthur Byne," 140–41. In 2024 Enric Mallorquí-Ruscalleda published that the staircase labeled "Calle del Agua" is the staircase in Princeton's collections. His article presents the provenance information that the Museum provided in 2020, which was taken from the ensemble's accession card and bibliographic reference to the 1928 plate: "House on Calle del Agua, Palma de Majorca; Arthur Byne, Madrid (until 1929); Baron Cassel van Doorn, Englewood, New Jersey (until 1955, gift of Baroness Cassel van Doorn to the Princeton University Art Museum)." As noted above, it is now known that the ensemble was sold in 1929 to William Randolph Hearst. See Enric Mallorquí-Ruscalleda, "From Palma to Princeton: Reconstruction and Translation of the (Lost) Gothic-Renaissance Staircase of Calle del Agua," *Mirabilia Journal* 38, no. 1 (2024): 360.
27. For information on the potential connection to the Nogués family, see Gabriel Alomar i Esteve and Antoni I. Alomar i Canyelles, *El patrimoni cultural de les Illes Balears: Idees per una política de defensa i protecció* (Institut d'Estudis Baleàrics, Palma, 1994), 65. The information regarding the potential origins of the "Calle del Agua" staircase is noted in a caption beneath a cropped image of Byne's 1928 drawing, but no citations are included. The authors of this publication incorrectly note that the elements from Can Ayamans were sold to the American collector Leon Levy (62).

For information on Costa's acquisition of a ceiling, see Albert Velasco Gonzàlez, "Josep Costa Ferrer (1876–1971), antiquari i agent del mercat de l'art entre Barcelona i Palma," in *Mercat de l'art, colleccionisme i museus 2023*, ed. B. Bassegoda and I. Domènech (Universitat Autònoma de Barcelona, Bellaterra; Consorci del Patrimoni de Sitges, 2024), 209.
28. Byne to Costa, May 10, 1929, Costa Archive, as cited by Merino de Cáceres and Martínez Ruiz, "Arthur Byne," 140. The original text is in Spanish and has been translated to English by this author: "A mano sus dos cartas de recién fecha manifestando el progreso hecho hasta la fecha con las piedras de la escalera; me alegro que hayan salido 5 tramos enteros.... En cuanto tenga Vd. todas las piedras en el suelo del local de embalaje haga el favor de avisarme. tengo que preparar algunos dibujos y al mismo tiempo ver si es factible combinar las piedras de la escalera que está arreglando Sacanell con las del patio."
29. Byne to William Randolph Hearst, September 12, 1929, JMP, box 45, folder 14; and Byne to Julia Morgan, November 1, 1929, JMP, box 45, folder 14.
30. Ripoll, "Notas sobre unas piedras viejas," unnumbered page between 268 and 269.
31. Museu de Mallorca, Palma, inv. nos. DA05/14/0018, DA05/14/0019, DA05/14/0020, DA05/14/0021, DA05/14/0023, DA05/14/0024, DA05/14/0025, DA05/14/0026. The uncertain origins of these elements are discussed by Capellà Galmés and Domenge i Mesquida, "La escalera," 404, fig. 14; and Guillem Rosselló, *Museo de Mallorca* (Ministerio de Educación y Ciencia, 1976), 47.
32. Rafael de Ysasi and G. Rosselló Bordoy, *Palma de antaño: A través de un cristal* (Olañeta, 1998), 99–100. This staircase was also mentioned by Capellà Galmés and Domenge i Mesquida, "La escalera," 402–3.
33. This image was first published by Capellà Galmés and Domenge i Mesquida, "La escalera," 402. Its source is not cited, but Magdalena de Quiroga Conrado is credited with finding it. Quiroga Conrado is currently conducting further research on the 1920s movement

and restoration of the staircase, which may be published at a later date.
34. Caldwell, "Spanish Stairs Treatment Report," 6; and additional discussion with Kelly Caldwell.
35. Caldwell, "Spanish Stairs Treatment Report," 19; and additional discussion with Kelly Caldwell.
36. Mallorquí-Ruscalleda, "From Palma to Princeton," 363. In this publication, the author notes generally that the staircase now at Princeton appears to have been reassembled. However, an original order is not proposed, and his analysis does not include important contextual details regarding the object's installation history in the United States. The author also states that the staircase now at Princeton was from a patio illustrated in J. B. Laurens, *Souvenirs d'un voyage d'art à l'Ile de Majorque* (Paris, 1840), plate 43. But the carved decorations on the staircase now at Princeton and on the staircase illustrated by Laurens do not match.
37. Mallorquí-Ruscalleda, "From Palma to Princeton," 363.
38. I am grateful to Cloe Cavero de Carondelet, Princeton University, for her additional thoughts and input on the translation of the staircase's inscription.
39. The Bronx inventory records of the International Studio Art Corporation are stored at the William Randolph Hearst Archive, Long Island University. The Princeton patio was registered in album 83, item no. 6, 19–22 (lot 275, nos. 1–65).
40. Enclosed sketches or photographs are mentioned in letters from Arthur Byne to Julia Morgan, March 25, April 8, and July 14, 1929, JMP, box 45, folder 14. I am grateful to Maryam Momeni of Special Collections and Archives at Cal Poly for her help determining that these enclosures were not located elsewhere in the archive.
41. Miller Druck & Co., Inc., "Alterations and Additions to Residence, 240 Broad Ave., Englewood, New Jersey" (1942), Curatorial File, y1955-3282, Princeton University Art Museum; and Pizzutello Stone Works, Inc., "Alt. & Add. To Residence, 240 Broad Ave., Englewood, N.J." (1942), Curatorial Files, y1955-3282, Princeton University Art Museum.
42. Pizzutello Stone Works, Inc., "Alt. & Add. To Residence."
43. Pizzutello Stone Works, Inc., "Alt. & Add. To Residence."
44. Carl Otto Kienbusch to Patrick J. Kelleher, August 19, 1963, Baroness Cassel van Doorn Donor File, Princeton University Art Museum.
45. Ernest T. DeWald to Arthur E. Fox, October 16, 1955, Princeton University, Office of the President Records: Robert F. Goheen (AC #193), box 515, folder 13, series 18.2: Van Doorn, Baroness Cassel, 1955.
46. Accession card, y1955-3282, Princeton University Art Museum.
47. Michael Morris, unpublished treatment documentation, 2010, Conservation Files, Princeton University Art Museum.
48. "Princeton Opens 53 Million Drive," *New York Times*, February 22, 1959, 73; and Douglas Martin, "Robert F. Goheen, Innovative Princeton President, Is Dead at 88," *New York Times*, April 1, 2008. During Goheen's tenure the University built or acquired thirty-eight new buildings, doubled the amount of indoor space, quadrupled the budget, and increased its staff.
49. Sara E. Bush, "An Art Museum for Princeton: The Early Years," *Record of the Art Museum, Princeton University* 55, no. 1/2 (1996): 97–100.
50. Kienbusch to Kelleher, August 19, 1963.
51. John G. Faron, untitled handwritten note to unknown recipient, April 10, 1962, Curatorial Files, y1955-3282, Princeton University Art Museum.
52. Copies of meeting minutes prepared by various representatives of Steinmann, Cain & White from 1960 to 1965 can be found in Office of Physical Planning Records, 1869–1994 (mostly 1946–1994), box 63, folder 3 (McCormick Hall Correspondence — Steinman [*sic*], Cain and White, 1960–1964), and folder 6 (Correspondence — Steinman [*sic*] and Cain, 1965–1966), Mudd Library, Princeton University. Copies are also located in Department of Art and Archaeology Records, 1882–2017 (mostly 1925–1981), AC140, box 2 (McCormick Hall Renovations, 1959–1966).
53. W. D. Vanderpool, copy of meeting minutes for "Princeton University: McCormick Hall," February 14, 1963, Office of Physical Planning Records, box 63, folder 3, 3.
54. Copy of purchase order sent from Princeton's Office of Physical Planning to Bohren's Moving & Storage, July 19, 1963, and copy of invoice from Bohren's Moving & Storage, July 22, 1963, Office of Physical Planning Records, box 63, folder 10 (A-1215 — McCormick Hall Additions).
55. Professor Richard Stillwell to R. L. Johnstone, Department of Art and Archaeology Records, box 8, unnumbered folder ("Remodeling and New Museum, 1930–1966).")
56. Alfred Rheinstein to John G.

Faron, February 4, 1964, Office of Physical Planning Records, box 63, folder 3.

57. Frances Follin Jones, "Objects and Material Belonging to the Art Museum Stored in 'The Big Study Room' on the Ground Floor of McCormick Hall, Listed by Their Official Inventory Numbers, March, 1964," Office of Physical Planning Records, box 62, folder 21 (Progress Photos 1965–66), 2.

58. John G. Faron, copy of meeting minutes for "Alterations & Additions to McCormick Hall, Princeton University," March 17, 1965, Department of Art and Archaeology Records, AC140, box 2 (McCormick Hall Renovations, 1959–1966), 3.

59. John G. Faron, copy of meeting minutes for "Alterations & Additions to McCormick Hall, Princeton University," December 9, 1964, Department of Art and Archaeology Records, AC140, box 2 (McCormick Hall Renovations, 1959–1966), 2.

60. John G. Faron, copy of meeting minutes for "Alterations & Additions to McCormick Hall, Princeton University," January 20, 1965, Department of Art and Archaeology Records, AC140, box 2 (McCormick Hall Renovations, 1959–1966), 1.

61. Faron, copy of meeting minutes for "Alterations & Additions to McCormick Hall, Princeton University," January 20, 1965, 3.

62. Alfred Rheinstein to Ricardo A. Mestres, December 21, 1965, Office of the President Records: Robert F. Goheen, AC193, box 367, folder 4, series 11.4 (McCormick Hall–Art and Archaeology and Marquand Library, 1962–1966).

63. Caldwell, "Spanish Stairs Treatment Report," 14; and additional discussion with Kelly Caldwell.

64. Jablonski Building Conservation, Inc., "Treatment Report: Pietro Lombardo Doorway y1950-22," October 2022, Conservation File, Princeton University Art Museum; and additional discussion with Mary Jablonski and Danielle Pape.

65. Rheinstein to John G. Faron, May 10, 1965, Office of Physical Planning Records, box 63, folder 3.

66. John G. Faron, copy of meeting minutes for "Alterations & Additions to McCormick Hall, Princeton University," May 26, 1965, Department of Art and Archaeology Records, AC140, box 2 (McCormick Hall Renovations, 1959–1966), 3.

67. Rheinstein to Faron, May 10, 1965.

68. Faron, copy of meeting minutes for "Alterations & Additions to McCormick Hall, Princeton University," March 17, 1965, 3.

69. John G. Faron, copy of meeting minutes for "Alterations & Additions to McCormick Hall, Princeton University," April 14, 1965, Department of Art and Archaeology Records, AC140, box 2 (McCormick Hall Renovations, 1959–1966), 2.

70. Kelleher to John Moran, Office of Physical Planning Records, box 63, folder 3.

71. Princeton University Art Museum, "New Princeton University Art Museum Envisioned as 'Cultural Gateway'; Architects Selected," press release, September 18, 2018, https://artmuseum.princeton.edu/about/press-room/press-release/new-princeton-university-art-museum-envisioned-cultural-gateway.

Acknowledgments

The collaborative research on Princeton's Mallorcan stairway and gallery presented in this volume has benefited from the expertise and generosity of individuals working across various disciplines. From the earliest phases of research on these architectural elements to our explorations of installation possibilities that reflected our new understanding of the elements' previous contexts, we received vital support from numerous colleagues at the Princeton University Art Museum. We are particularly indebted to James Steward, Nancy A. Nasher–David J. Haemisegger, Class of 1976, Director; Chris Newth, senior associate director for exhibitions and collections; Juliana Ochs Dweck, chief curator; and Bart Devolder, chief conservator. Michael Jacobs, senior gallery designer and manager of exhibitions services, was a crucial partner in thinking through questions of display in the Museum's new building. The successful installation of the stairway and gallery was achieved through the contributions of Todd Baldwin, manager of exhibition preparation and art handling; Katie Getchell, senior project manager; Christopher Gorzelnik, senior lighting technician; Laura Hahn, senior manager, museum projects and strategic initiatives; Alexia Hughes, chief registrar and manager of collections; Carol Rossi, registrar; and Lindsey Young-Lockett, project collections associate. This work was done in close collaboration with colleagues in the Office of Capital Projects at Princeton University, including Dan Bolohan and Solace Burkhimer, project managers; Sara Cicerone, former director of construction; Jane Curry, senior program manager; Dale Edghill, senior project manager; and George Morris and Andrew Triggas, field managers.

The conservation treatment and installation of the stairway and gallery required an array of specialists. We are especially grateful to the team at EverGreene Architectural Arts, particularly Kelly Caldwell, whose leadership and expertise were integral, as well as Silvia Callegari, Katharine George, Brooke Russell, Meghan Page, Mirta Vidal, Mark Rabinowitz, Alex Munn, and Rachel Evans. Our thanks also to Darrel Isaacs, David Etchison, Delbert Carvajal, Luis Pineda, Mayron Pineda, Juan Castro, and Mario Garza from Standard Restoration and Waterproofing; Gillian Love, Gary Strand, and Bernardo J. Carrera from Simpson Gumpertz & Heger; Clayton Vogel from Artist & Title; Marc McQuade and Matthew Storrie, formerly with Adjaye Associates; and Wendy Cronk and Erin Flynn from Cooper Robertson.

Research on these elements took us to historic sites, museums, libraries, and archives from California to Mallorca. Our archival research was graciously facilitated by the staffs at Mudd Library, Princeton University; Special Collections and Archives at the Robert E. Kennedy Library, California Polytechnic State University, San Luis Obispo; and Bancroft Library, University of California, Berkeley; and by Heather Hesse and Catherine Larkin at Archives & Special Collections, Long Island University. Patrick Lenaghan made photographs of Arthur Byne's 1915 expedition to Mallorca available for consultation and publication and offered his insights into Byne and Mildred Stapley's relationship with the Hispanic Society. Mary L. Levkoff shared her unparalleled knowledge of William Randolph Hearst's collecting and archives; Cara O'Brien and Carrie Arnold at Hearst San Simeon State Historical Monument arranged for a private tour of the site focused on Byne and answered numerous questions regarding Hearst and San Simeon. William B. Russell Jr. first made us aware of the Cassel van Doorn family album with photographs of their Englewood, New Jersey, estate and introduced us to the youngest daughter of the baron and baroness, Anne-Marie de Rivera, and her daughter Maria de

Rivera, who shared their recollections and photographs of the baron and baroness. Meredith Hanna Noorda provided crucial research support, particularly regarding the Cassel van Doorn family, and the Museum's Curator of Provenance MaryKate Cleary lent her expertise in Nazi-era provenance research as we pieced together the history of the Cassel van Doorn collections. Cloe Cavero de Carondelet analyzed the inscriptions on Princeton's stairway, and Costanza Beltrami suggested bibliographic material for the history of Mallorcan architecture. Museum Information Coordinator Sarah Brown and Research Curator of European Painting and Sculpture emerita Betsy Rosasco shared their deep knowledge of the Princeton University Art Museum's institutional history.

In addition, several individuals provided invaluable support in translating our research on the Mallorcan stairway and gallery—as well as its conservation treatment and installation—into this handsome volume. Cristina Aldrich and Pamela Patton offered extensive feedback on our essays that immeasurably enriched them. Managing Editor Anna Brouwer deftly shepherded the editorial and design process, and Assistant Editor Kate Justement coordinated images. Manager of Foundation and Government Relations Courtney Lacy assisted with fundraising. The Museum's imaging team of Jeff Evans, manager of visual resources, and Joseph Hu, visual imaging specialist, along with former Museum photographer Emile Askey, documented the stairway and gallery's deinstallation, conservation, and installation in the new building. Their photographs are featured throughout this publication. Our thanks to copy editor Karen Jacobson for her careful attention to our essay texts and to Dianne Woo for her diligent proofreading. Joseph Cho and Stefanie Lew of Binocular thoughtfully developed the elegant design of this volume and the new series it inaugurates. The color separations and printing were overseen by Massimo Tonolli and Silvia Zanetti at Trifolio.

From Palma to Princeton was made possible in part by the Andrew W. Mellon Foundation Publications Fund, Princeton University Art Museum, and the Barr Ferree Foundation Fund for Publications, Department of Art & Archaeology, Princeton University.

Alexandra Letvin
Duane Wilder, Class of 1951,
Associate Curator of European Art

Elena Torok
Associate Objects Conservator

Image Credits

Architectural Record Archives: figs. 14, 15
Courtesy Archives of American Art, Smithsonian Institution, Washington, DC. Andrew Carnduff Ritchie papers, 1907–1983: fig. 36
Photo by Emile Askey: figs. 55, 66, 67
Courtesy Bison Archives/Marc Wanamaker. Photo by Irvin Willat: fig. 18
Reproduced from Arthur Byne and Mildred Stapley Byne, *Majorcan Houses and Gardens: A Spanish Island in the Mediterranean* (W. Helburn, 1928), plates 159, 160. Photo by Roel Muñoz: figs. 8, 26, 56 (left, detail)
California Polytechnic State University, San Luis Obispo. Special Collections and Archives, Julia Morgan Papers: figs. 12, 24, 25; photo by Harold Wesley Truesdale: fig. 19
Reproduced from Álvaro Campaner y Fuertes, *Cronicon Mayoricense: Noticias y relaciones históricas de Mallorca desde 1229 a 1800* (Palma de Mallorca, 1881), plate VII: fig. 51
Courtesy Cassel van Doorn Archive: figs. 28, 29, 31, 32
Courtesy Catedral de Mallorca: fig. 9
Courtesy Consell de Mallorca. Arxiu del So i de la Imatge de Mallorca, Col·lecció Cabot Umbert: fig. 47
Costa Archive: fig. 27
Digital Document Repository, Universitat Autònoma de Barcelona Library. Reproduced from Genaro Pérez Villaamil and Patricio de la Escosura, *España artística y monumental: Vistas y descripcion de los sitios y monumentos mas notables de España*, vol. 2 (Paris, 1844), 38: fig. 23
Photo by Jeffrey Evans: figs. 42, 43, 44, 45, 61, 62, 63, 64
Photo by EverGreene Architectural Arts: figs. 41, 59
Courtesy Hispanic Society Museum & Library, New York. Photo by Patrick Lenaghan: fig. 17
Photo by Joseph Hu: figs. 3, 4, 30, 33, 34, 39, 40, 52, 54, 56 (right), 60, 69, 70; pp. 72–86
Courtesy Isabella Stewart Gardner Museum, Boston. Photo by Sean Dungan: fig. 16
Library of Congress, Washington, DC. Prints and Photographs Division: fig. 20
José María Marco family album: fig. 48
Reproduced from José Miguel Merino de Cáceres and María José Martínez Ruiz, “Arthur Byne, Mildred Stapley, José Costa y el patio de la Casa Ayamans (Palma de Mallorca): Detalles de un despojo artístico en el contexto de la promoción turística balear,” *Espacio, tiempo y forma* 7, no. 10 (2022), figura 7: fig. 46
The Metropolitan Museum of Art, New York: figs. 10, 11
Photo by Rolf Müller/Wikimedia Commons: fig. 21
Courtesy Museum of Mallorca. Photo by J. Joan Tous: fig. 53
Panther Media Global/Alamy: fig. 5
Reproduced from Pablo Piferrer and José María Quadrado, *España: Sus monumentos y artes, su naturaleza e historia*, vol. 27: *Islas Baleares* (Barcelona, 1888), 653: fig. 1
Courtesy Princeton University Library. Department of Special Collections: figs. 2, 68
Reproduced from Archduke Ludwig Salvator, *La ciudad de Palma. Parte de la obre Las Baleares descritas por la palabra y el grabado* (Mossén Alcover, 1954), 74–75: figs. 49, 50
Photo © Frank Schulenburg/Wikimedia Commons: fig. 22
Shutterstock (2450963013): fig. 6
Smithsonian American Art Museum, Washington, DC. Peter A. Juley & Son Collection, Photograph Study Collection. Photo by Peter A. Juley & Son: fig. 13
Diagram by Elena Torok: fig. 7
University of Alberta Library Internet Archive Digital Collections: fig. 37
Photo by Bruce M. White: fig. 65
Reproduced from Rafael de Ysasi and G. Rosselló Bordoy, *Palma de antaño: A través de un cristal* (José J. de Olañeta, 1998), 99–100. © Heirs of Rafael de Ysasi: figs. 57, 58

STUDY ROOM *From Palma to Princeton: Unraveling the Mystery of a Mallorcan Stairway* launches the new book series Study Room, created to provide focused, interdisciplinary investigations of essential works in the Princeton University Art Museum's collections. The series will reflect the collections' scope and depth and the diverse approaches that can productively be brought to bear on the study of important works of art.

This publication is made possible in part by the Andrew W. Mellon Foundation Publications Fund, Princeton University Art Museum, and the Barr Ferree Foundation Fund for Publications, Department of Art & Archaeology, Princeton University.

Published by the
Princeton University Art Museum
Princeton, NJ 08544-1018
artmuseum.princeton.edu

Project editor: Anna Brouwer
Copy editor: Karen Jacobson
Image coordinator: Kate Justement
Proofreader: Dianne Woo

Series design, book design, and composition: Binocular, New York

Color separations, printing, and binding: Trifolio, Verona

Typeset in Comenia Serif and Comenia Sans, and printed on Munken Lynx 130 gsm and Symbol Tatami 135 gsm

Distributed by
Princeton University Press
41 William Street
Princeton, NJ 08540-5237
99 Banbury Road
Oxford OX2 6JX
press.princeton.edu

GPSR authorized representative:
Easy Access System Europe
Mustamäe tee 50
10621 Tallinn, Estonia
gpsr.requests@easproject.com

ISBN: 978-0-691-97890-1
ISBN: 978-0-691-97892-5 (e-book)

Library of Congress Control Number: 2025941516

British Library Cataloging-in-Publication Data is available

Printed and bound in Italy
10 9 8 7 6 5 4 3 2 1